Bitter Experience Has Taught Me

Nicholas Lezard is a weekly contributor to the *Guardian*'s book pages, and writes the 'Down and Out in London' column in the *New Statesman*, from which this book has been adapted, and bits and bobs for the *Independent* and the London *Evening Standard*. He wrote the *Guardian*'s notorious 'Slack Dad' column for years and was, for a decade, the *Independent on Sunday*'s radio critic. But, as he has discovered, nothing lasts for ever.

by the same author

THE NOLYMPICS

Bitter Experience Has Taught Me

NICHOLAS LEZARD

faber and faber

First published in 2013
by Faber and Faber Limited
Bloomsbury House
74–77 Great Russell Street
London WC1B 3DA

Typeset by Faber and Faber Ltd
Printed and bound by CPI Group (UK) Ltd, Croydon, CR0 4YY

All rights reserved
© Nicholas Lezard, 2013

The right of Nicholas Lezard to be identified as author
of this work has been asserted in accordance with Section 77
of the Copyright, Designs and Patents Act 1988

*This book is sold subject to the condition that it shall not,
by way of trade or otherwise, be lent, resold, hired out
or otherwise circulated without the publisher's prior consent
in any form of binding or cover other than that in which it
is published and without a similar condition including
this condition being imposed on the subsequent purchaser*

A CIP record for this book
is available from the British Library

ISBN 978-0-571-29916-4

For my children

I solve it thus. And for those other faults of barbarism, Doric dialect, extemporanean style, tautologies, apish imitation, a rhapsody of rags gathered together from several dunghills, excrements of authors, toys and fopperies confusedly tumbled out, without art, invention, judgment, wit, learning, harsh, raw, rude, fantastical, absurd, insolent, indiscreet, ill-composed, indigested, vain, scurrile, idle, dull, and dry; I confess all ('tis partly affected), thou canst not think worse of me than I do of myself. 'Tis not worth the reading, I yield it, I desire thee not to lose time in perusing so vain a subject, I should be peradventure loath myself to read him or thee so writing; 'tis not *operae, pretium*. All I say is this, that I have precedents for it.

ROBERT BURTON, *The Anatomy of Melancholy*

Autobiography is only to be trusted when it reveals something disgraceful.

GEORGE ORWELL

Prologue: The Hovel

So, like a school term, new life begins in September. The intervening period from the end of June had been horrible: like an anti-holiday. Living with someone who has given you your marching orders is trying, to put it mildly. Particularly if you don't feel like marching. Had we stuck it out until 28 November, we would have survived, although in the latter stages 'endured' is perhaps the better word, twenty years of being together. This is quite the long haul in this day and age, and I had hoped that there would be enough good juju about the anniversary to assure further continuation. But this is almost certainly wishful thinking. 'I've changed, you haven't,' was one devastating mantra I kept hearing towards the end, unanswerable really. Also: 'You never do anything you don't want to do.' Well, all I could think of in response to that, after a little shrug suggesting that there were, in fact, many things that I did which I would have preferred not to, was 'One tries one's best.' And, no, I had not changed, or not much. I had, if you want to look at it one way, changed back: I had given up the, for me, demeaning and soul-crushing office job at, of all places, British Telecom and become a freelance writer: earning enough, miraculously, to raise three children and live in a three-bedroomed house in Shepherd's Bush, but living, for all other intents, the life of a student. Reading books and then writing about them. Or being asked to have opinions about Things and writing them down. And later, in a further excellent development, listening to the radio and then writing about that. And all for money.

The interesting thing about all these requirements is that, thanks to the invention of the laptop, not only the research but the writing can be done in bed. The commute to the office involved nothing more than leaning over the side of the bed and picking up a book from the floor. Or, in the case of the radio criticism, sometimes going all the way down to the kitchen, retrieving the Sony, and taking it back upstairs and switching it on.

I suppose such fortuitous idleness comes at a price: that of one's own maturity. Be careful what you wish for, and I had wished for nothing so intensely as a life in which I would be spared the horrors of the early-morning commute on the crowded tube, the snatched bacon sandwich from the café over the road, the office canteen lunch, the scratch around the revolted cerebellum for the glib slogan for the marketing department, and the early-evening commute back on the crowded tube. To revert to the undergraduate existence and to be paid for it was, for me, to be as happy as a pig in shit. When that is accompanied by the small sprinkling of glamour that attaches itself to the word 'writer' then pretty much all one's selfish needs have been addressed, and when that happens, complacency sets in, and if one is also deficient in ambition then the soul stagnates. The stagnation and complacency then spread to the business of maintaining a marriage. Add this to an already rock-solid aversion to the conventional trimmings of domesticity – the purgatorial trips to Homebase and Ikea, the visits to the in-laws – and the future is never really in doubt. So I find myself, eventually, sacked, taking what I only absolutely have to take with me in a series of bin liners to a temporary home. I have no experience of this kind of thing, not even second-hand. I am, with one exception, the first of my circle to have been placed in this situation. The culture is full of stories of men putting a brave face on things and convincing themselves that they have found a new life, a reversion to groovy bachelorhood in their middle years. Which are, let us not kid ourselves, the beginning of the end years. And the reality of the situation is rather more like that as suffered by Milhouse's father in *The Simpsons*: a shameful block of rotting single-room apartments called 'Bachelor Heights', whose sign outside, regularly reverting to zero, lists the number of days since its last suicide, and from where, at night, you can hear the sound of men crying themselves to sleep.

Well, at some point, sooner rather than later, although it takes me a very painful three months, you have to find somewhere else to live. It is my old friend Razors who tells me about the Hovel. I had been staying at my brother's for a while, in one of those hidden folds of London that not even estate agents have bothered to give a name. This extra-dimensional place is in some ghost zone between the tube stations of Neasden and Dollis Hill, and while the house itself is very well kept, the neighbourhood is unprepossessing, and the domesticity of the place is a constant reminder of what I have lost. I hole out at my friend Tom's place in North Devon, where we would all holiday: I look after the chickens, the pony, the cats, the Rayburn. It is a ramshackle place, utterly unpretentious and genuine, a healing environment, and crammed with good books, but it is not my own, and Tom and his wife Vic have three children of their own, and after a while, once I have worked out I am not going to kill myself after all, it is time to move back to the city of my birth. The dog returns to his vomit as the fool to his folly.

The Hovel is a place whose purpose is now, I gather, for displaced or errant husbands, occupying the first, second and third floors of an 1850 house near Baker Street. This is good news. But it is, when I first inspect it, the end of the good news. (I remember when my wife and I had to make the move from the tiny, mushroom-infested basement studio flat where we lived together in Bayswater to a larger place over the psychic barrier of the Shepherd's Bush roundabout. I remember turning round in my seat to look out of the back windows of the rented van we were able to fit all our crap in in one go, and vowing: 'I'll be back.' By which I meant my spiritual home: the central zone of London as determined by British Telecom, or the Circle Line of the London Underground. But I never imagined I'd be back like *this*.)

For the first part of the bad news, apart from the fact that I'm going to have to live away from the family home, is that Razors is moving out soon, for what I hope is a short time, but maybe not. Everything is up in the air, unsettlingly. But I gather that I will, for most of the time, be the sole inhabitant, at least until a new tenant arrives. I am not sure I am going to like this. Going from living with four other people to living with none seems to be rather an abrupt transition and I wonder how I will be able to take it. I have also never, except for short periods, lived in a house where I am neither married nor intimately related to any of the other occupants.

I soon discover why it is so much more affordable than even a one-bed flat in Shepherd's Bush.*

---

* I have no desire to buy anywhere, as that would entail selling the house, and I don't think the children would like that. Moving house induces in me profound sensations of terror and regret, a condition known to the psychiatric profession as tropophobia, which is also the term for the fear of making changes. So if my children are anything like me, and there is every reason to suspect that they are at least fifty per cent like me, they, too, would suffer from this syndrome.

The door opens onto a plain corridor, long enough for a couple of bikes to park themselves end to end, but not much else. The floorboards are non-professionally painted a pleasing burnt red, reminding me of so many student and post-student shared houses. Thanks to a supporting beam having been removed in the 1960s, the floors sag in the middle, like the stomach of a portly old man who's untied his cummerbund. The stairs up to the bedrooms on the second floor slope at an angle of about ten degrees from the horizontal, the floor of the kitchen the same in the other direction; later, when I come to live here and fry an egg, it pools in the corner of the pan and assumes the shape of a crescent moon.

It is quickly apparent that this is almost the complete antithesis of a family home.

The only rooms you can sit or lie down in face on to the front. Unless you want to sit or lie down in either of the two bathrooms, neither of which have seen a decorator's hand since Abba won the Eurovision Song Contest with 'Waterloo', and are correspondingly decrepit (and, although lying down in a bathroom is not something I have done since the great head-spin incident of 1988, a look at their dimensions suggests I would have to adopt the foetal position if I wanted to do such an ignoble thing). The kitchen cabinets have likewise not been upgraded since, I would say, 1972, and even then only in the most cursory and rudimentary fashion. There is a newish – 1985?

1990? – electric hob, but I don't like electric hobs as I fancy myself as pretty good at cooking; on the other hand, I don't feel like eating anything. It's not just the sadness. It's also the weird feeling of cooking with implements which are not mine. For these things are not mine. Nothing is now really mine.

The living room is high-ceilinged, but dingy, and not too large. The off-cream wallpaper, thickened with ancient paint, peels off the walls. A possibly Victorian chaise longue sits frailly, pointedly ignoring the 1970s squishy vinylette sofa on the opposite wall. The shelves opposite the bookcase contain dusty knick-knacks and various bottles of spirits, and you know without having to investigate that the drinkable ones will be empty (lacklustre investigation confirms this). But there will be loads of ouzo, schnapps and other poisonous muck brought back from holidays. As for the bookshelf, there are a couple of rows of drama and the odd thing by Simon Callow, suggesting at some point a professional and thoughtful relationship to the theatre. Underneath are three or four rows of inspirational, high-end hippy. Two copies, for some reason, of *Blackfoot Physics*. *The Teachings of Don Carlos*. *The Joy of Success* is a title that would appear to operate some light years away from my own circumstances, and *Your Best Year Yet* even manages to elicit a hollow laugh from me, as does John Harvey-Jones's *Making It Happen*. A book called *Making It Unhappen* might have more appeal, but I suspect that has yet to be written, unless this one, under another title, is it.*

I inspect the available bedrooms. One is so narrow I could, I think, suspend myself above the floor by freezing myself in mid-star-jump and pressing against the opposing walls with my hands and feet.

---

* Reading matter is important to me – as it should be: I'm a book critic. I suspect I'm the last one on either side of the Atlantic, and possibly in the world, whose primary source of income is book reviewing. But when disaster of the soul strikes, I retreat into the comforts of genre fiction, or the books of my childhood. When things are bad, I read James Bond novels or Sherlock Holmes. When they are very bad, I read P. G. Wodehouse. When they are absolutely appalling, I reread *The Lord of the Rings*, which may make some of my colleagues raise their eyebrows, disdainful as most of them are about the works of J. R. R. Tolkien, but my excuse is that in this I am trying to recapture my childhood, specifically around when I was eleven years old, when everything was *all right*. (Well, it wasn't, not really, not idyllically, but then childhood assumes this character for the distressed adult; a time of zero responsibility, when one's only real anxieties were, it seems in retrospect, nebulously existential. Which they weren't, of course. But it was *all right* when I was lost in a book, especially an epic set in an imaginary past when there was still magic in the world.) Wodehouse, at the moment, is causing me a lot of problems. His world is indeed Edenic, prelapsarian; but I find myself taking his deliberately silly love-plots seriously, and becoming enormously fretful about the prospects of his characters' problematic engagements. Please, I say to myself, the tears welling in my eyes, let it all work out for Bingo Little. And Bertie, what is so bad about Florence Cray? At least you will have in her a woman who cares whether you are alive or dead.

The other has a vestigial desk – a thin black slab of chipboard wedged in the space between the wall and the walled-over fireplace. A bare overhead bulb, a bare standard lamp. The bed would appear to be a sofa, again of 1970s vintage – I begin to notice a recurring motif in the interior decor – which has not been folded out. When folded out it would be not quite as large as the bed I had slept in since childhood (and which has been inherited by my eldest child). Like the room Watt moves into in Beckett's novel, it contains no information. The only decorations are a Kandinsky print from the Pompidou Centre which I can't identify, but which is, while not one of his best, good enough for me to work out instantly that I will never bother to replace it, and a photograph of the Northern Lights from a newspaper glued onto a piece of thin card. The only book on the shelf is a small motivational booklet for businessmen. A Yale key on a ring with a broken fob lies next to it. A pack of cards, a small stopped clock. A clasp knife with a wooden haft, its single blade rusty and blunt, useless for purposes of self-immolation, threat, or even, as I eventually discover, cutting string.

The bathroom, to the connoisseur of dilapidation, offers rich rewards. How, first, to describe its colour scheme? Something like peach, yet no peach with such a colour ever grew on earth. It is mixed with some kind of brown. I need not, by now, tell you in which decade it saw its last renovation. There is a black bin liner filled with something next to the sink. It doesn't look as though it's going anywhere in a hurry. There is a bath which looks, and indeed turns out to be, patently unusable. The bathroom cabinet is just *wrong*. It is full of temporary stuff that has become permanent. What use, I wonder, will I have, never having impregnated one before, for a Mosquito Net Reimpregnation Kit? (I still haven't thrown it out, and it may fool visitors into thinking I am an intrepid tropical explorer.) And what is Napier's Plantain and Eyebright Compound for? Its ingredients distract me: Extracts of Bloodroot, Pokeroot, Eyebright . . . I am advised that if symptoms persist, I should consult a Medical Herbalist. But what symptoms are these? Who suffered from them? And who used the surely-by-now-toxic salon-sized tub of shampoo? Will I, too, leave nothing more consequential behind me for the next nomadic inhabitant?

In short, the whole place looks like it could do with a woman's touch.

Actually, it looks like it could do with a man's touch, too.

It could also do with a child's touch: my children's, specifically, and I dare not think about them, or what they might be thinking, for that way lies terror and insanity.

It is the saddest place I have ever seen.

So as I trudge away from it, my heart is heavy, for although it is in W1 it is very depressing when compared to the home I have left. Which may itself have been a shambles – the cat, for instance, has taken a (perfectly understandable) dislike to the wallpaper, and great fronds of it hang off the hallway walls; the kitchen is usually colder than the outside temperature; and the boiler is going to blow up any day now; but it was my home. It was where I lived. It was where I belonged. It was what kept the tropophobia at bay. And I distinctly – no, vividly – recall having a lot more stuff at my old place.

And so I find myself inhabiting a realm which I had hitherto complacently consigned to the realm of nightmare: scary, yet unreal. It is now real; this is my reality. That it all feels very unreal indeed is no consolation, but it may, I suspect, be the only one available to me for the time being.

But impermanence is the presiding atmosphere. I know that all flesh is as grass, and *où sont les neiges d'antan* and all that, and that no one steps into the same river twice, but it is undeniable that the Hovel does not feel like *home*. Not the home I have been expelled from, the home whose floors I sanded, whose skirting boards I painted, sometimes even in colours of my own choice, whose every inch I know. I find myself looking at the pepper mill. By the time this needs refilling, I think to myself . . . What? I'll be back with my family? I see toilet roll in Waitrose. If I buy a big bag of nine ultra-soft I get three extra free. If I consider the economics, this is important, for money is hard to come by. But twelve toilet rolls? Surely I'll have moved out, or be dead, long before I've run through them all?

So this is the set-up. I am, on balance, feeling fairly sorry for myself, as you might have gathered. But, as I leave the Hovel after picking up my keys before my tenancy officially begins, I walk down the other end of the street to explore my surroundings. I see a chemist whose exterior boasts that it has been there since 1814; and the exterior, gilt and ornate, with an amazing lamp hanging on the corner, seems to have been preserved since then. I see a pub, pillar-box red with eccentric little ornaments in the windows (tin soldiers, medals); the street opens up suddenly into an almost Italianate square whose northern side is taken up with a classically pleasing Hawksmoor-esque church – with, I note, a working clock which chimes the quarter hours. It is a beautiful day in late summer, shirt-sleeve weather. The area is classy, sure, but with a villagey atmosphere; it has a discrete *identity*. And then, turning back, I notice the most wonderful thing of all: a branch of Majestic, not forty yards from my front door.

So maybe things might just turn out all right after all.

After this, I more or less go into a coma, and we emerge, after Razors' welcome and fortuitous return some time later, in March 2009.

1

It's really beginning to look as though I have survived the winter. It was touch and go. This is a trying season for the man exiled from his hearth; not only because it is cold and dark, and stepping outside for a cigarette is unpleasant, but because you are meant to be in your own, original home, cosy and protected from the wolves, when the sun sets at four. You also have the added burden of the Separated Parent Christmas which, as I was once warned by one who knew, was 'the real sucking-shit-through-a-straw time for the divorced man'.

Last year I was saved from suicide not only by recalling E. M. Cioran's aperçu that there is no point in killing yourself, because by the time you do it it is, by definition, *too late*, but also by an unlikely romance with the Pole, a woman of awe-inspiring beauty driven to distraction by her right-wing colleagues. I won her heart by writing for the *Guardian* and correctly guessing which socialist heroine she had been named after. (There aren't that many.) That gave me a warm glow for a couple of months until I blew it in a rather instructive way. After gently ribbing her for her habit of going to the gym (which, like Homer Simpson, I prefer to pronounce with a hard 'g' and to rhyme with 'time'), she asked me if I would still fancy her if she were twenty kilos heavier. I'm more of an imperial weights and measures guy than a metric one, but twenty kilos did seem like an awful lot of weight to put on even in theory and so, rashly assuming that I was being tested on my honesty rather than on my gallantry, I said, 'No'. I didn't see anything much of her after that. Gentlemen, take heed. What's annoying is that if she'd had said ten kilos I'd have said, 'Yes'. And I am haunted by the fear that she might actually have said 'ten' in the first place. We were in a noisy pub, and my hearing isn't getting any better.

This year I have been saved by the presence in the Hovel of my good friend Razors. This is a man I have known for some years. We are mentally attuned, we discovered early on, to the degree that when we realised that we liked each other enough to give each other Christmas presents, we gave each other identical bottles of Lagavulin without any prior consultation. It was morphic resonance pure and simple. Or telepathy. Or something. In the months we have been living together I cannot recall, despite extraordinarily straitened financial circumstances, the kind that drive a wedge between the happiest of married couples, a single trivial argument, let alone a serious one – and he's a Spurs fan. He is certainly an improvement on the previous occupant of the Hovel, a serious-minded and taciturn Buddhist called Tim, who would pointedly, and with considerably more effort than he was saving himself, lift out every unwashed item of crockery from the sink which he had not himself soiled, not even pouring out the water from the bowls. Remarkably, his assertion of the demarcation lines of washing-up duties applied even if there was only a single spoon in the sink. He and Razors overlapped for a while, but not for long, particularly after Razors made his own point by returning the unwashed plates to the sink and then carefully smashing them to bits. Tim got the message and went off to live on a barge. I am sure he is much happier for it, and I wish him well.

But living with Razors has been something of a revelation. At first glance, we are the Odd Couple – I look like some poncey, stringy French intellectual while he looks as though his business name is, well, 'Razors', but he can actually complete the *Guardian* crossword and correctly answers many of the questions on *University Challenge*, although not as many as I do, of course. Unlike some marriages, our relationship is characterised by and composed of myriad small mutual kindnesses. We buy each other soup. We watch *Coronation Street* together. Why had no one told me about this television programme before? It is excellent. We even do each other's washing up. If I come back in the evening to discover that he has drunk three bottles of wine at a sitting, I do not berate him for alcoholism and break down in tears asking, rhetorically, What I Have Done to Deserve

This and arrange an Intervention, but instead cheerfully call him a greedy pig and look forward to his replenishing the stocks.

In short, I have gone back from being a family man to being a student. The parallels are uncanny. I looked up from my book; here I am again, poring over Samuel Beckett with a pencil in my hand. The only differences are that I'm being paid for it, my hair is a lot greyer, and I've got Haydn on in the background instead of Joy Division. The dog returns to his vomit as the fool to his folly; but, dammit, I *like* reading Beckett (that life at the moment resembles nothing so much as an indoor version of *Waiting for Godot* has its own piquancy).

And winter is being chased away. The very angle of the sun on the streets confirms this, gives us heart. The local, worryingly closed for a while, has reopened under new ownership, for which I thank Providence on bended knees. Soon we will be able to stretch out at full length on the Duke's outside benches, and listen to the church clock count off the quarter hours of our pleasantly futile lives.

*

It was watching Jeremy Paxman's programme about the Victorians, I remember, that gave me particular pause for thought. The bit that would have spooked most people – for when this came out, the recession was beginning to both bite and alarm – would have been the stuff about the workhouse. The Victorians, explained Paxman, believed that if you were unemployed it was Your Own Fault and the idle and profligate had only themselves to blame. Which, of course, is the core belief behind much of the Right's political discourse.

'Idle and profligate'. That was the kind of language they used back then, and having been called idle and profligate, or closely related variations thereof, for much of my life, I can't help thinking that the shadow of the workhouse looms over me, even though these days the idleness is forced upon me and the profligacy – well, the profligacy isn't that; it's just necessary expenditure. I know this because I had to fill in a form at Brent Magistrates' Court, and they wanted to know what I was spending, and how much I was earning, because they wanted to know how much they could fine me for neglecting to beep my Oyster card when travelling on a bendy bus to the British Library.

We're quite a numerous crew, we bendy-bus defaulters. Arrive at the Magistrates' Court and approach the security guard with any kind of hesitation, and he will say, 'Bendy bus?' You will nod, and, after the business with the metal detector, he will say, with the air of a man who has said this many times in the past, and will say so many more times in the future, that you are to go up to the second floor, Court 4. (Or whatever.)

Being done for such a footling crime, I reflected, represented A New Low. When I think of all the things they could get me for . . . I imagine this was how Al Capone felt, when he was pinched for tax evasion: indignant and foolish. Still, the list pinned up outside the courtroom goes all the way down to the floor, and while most people just plead guilty from home and forget about it, I felt that a trip to Neasden in the freezing drizzle was exactly the thing to buck me up. Besides, I had nothing else on, and I wanted to see what my fellow criminals looked like.

You are given a form to fill in which asks you how much you spend and how much you earn. I have always been rather cavalier about the whole earning/spending business; as long as bailiffs are not actually hammering on your door, you're fine. The interesting thing about this form, though, was that it suggested that the courts are rather more forgiving than the Inland Revenue as to what constitutes a legitimate expense. You are invited, for instance, to say how much you spend on clothes per month. Mindful of the fact that the last time I spent anything on clothes for myself was in the spring of 2007, yet anxious not to look like some kind of weirdo, I put £5 per month down as a token sum.

They also ask you how much you spend on food, alcohol and tobacco. I decided that the best thing to do would be to deduct the £5 I had claimed as my clothing allowance from my drinks bill. It still came to a horrendous amount, so I revised that down in case they thought I was an alcoholic. As for food – how much does one spend on food? All I know is that the last time I found myself in a supermarket, I had to remind myself that I couldn't actually afford mayonnaise. When I eventually tot up my expenses and compare them against what for want of a better word we shall call my income, I muse idly (and perhaps profligately) whether the courts won't fine me: they'll give me a grant.

And so this is what it has come to, I think to myself; I am forty-five years old, I am sleeping on a fold-out sofa, I can't afford mayonnaise unless I give up wine, which is out of the question, I share a house which sags so much in the middle that one doubts its stability and – as a result of brooding about these things instead of beeping my Oyster card – I am about to get a criminal record. I am turning, ahead of schedule, into Ed Reardon.

There are, of course, plenty of people in worse circumstances, particularly nowadays. And there is much to console myself with. I may no longer have a cat but the hovel I live in has several friendly mice I can play with; the pub down the road cashes cheques and the girl who works in the local Majestic is of surpassing charm. I forbear to ask the magistrate if there is a workhouse he could send me to. It is a consolation, I have to admit, that some time after this the last bendy bus was seen on London's streets. Sit long enough by the river, as the saying goes, and the body of your enemy will float by. Or, in this case, roll by, clogging up the traffic and snaring the dishonest or the forgetful for one last time.

*

On a whim, I ask my editors to put, beneath the gap where my column in a magazine used to be until the week before, the words 'Nicholas Lezard is unwell'. My many thanks to all the readers (not a *huge* number, I gather) who enquired after my health when they saw this. I was not, in fact, unwell; I had been rested for a week because the magazine was in the hands of a guest editor, and, as I have since come to learn, when there is a guest editor in town, I am sent to sit on the Naughty Step – *even if I have not been naughty*. The rubric was a conscious *hommage* to Jeffrey Bernard, who used to write a column called 'Low Life' at the magazine's deadly rival, the *Spectator*. As it happens, I used to hang out with Bernard, to the point that he had the sauce to pinch a girlfriend off me; she came back after a brief interval, during which she had discovered that diabetic alcoholics who drink a bottle of vodka a day can have problems in the sack. But that's another story for another day.

As to my unwellness, I have to say that, compared to my days in the family home, I am now astonishingly healthy. This may come as a surprise to those who have received calls from me saying I have been too unwell to do X, or Y; I will now come clean and say that almost all the time this has either been because the damage was self-inflicted the night before, or because I simply didn't feel like doing X, or Y. Genuinely blameless illness has struck me down for a total of probably five or six days in the last twenty-one months – and that's including one three-day bout of flu, the kind that was putting everyone else out of action for two weeks at a time.

Of course, this is physical illness we're talking about here. The first three or four months after I moved into the Hovel were spent pretty much in their entirety crying in bed, which I suppose counts as debility of a kind, but at least I could rouse myself enough to get my contracted work done. I have since learned that depression can manifest itself either as insomnia or its opposite, hypersomnia. I can warmly recommend the latter for the man in a crisis. The great thing about hypersomnia is that it builds up into a state that is more or less like the kind of suspended animation that some scientists recommend as the only solution for manned interstellar travel. Sleeping a lot, I discovered, tends to make you more sleepy; by the time you really hit your stride, you're spending about twenty-three hours a day in bed.

You do have to get out and about, though, but the other pleasant effect of hypersomnia is its Dorian Gray-like effect on the ageing process. I know this is tempting the Fates horribly, but I am looking rather well considering my age and what I do with myself (later on, I learn from an article in the *New Scientist* that sleeping a lot prevents obesity, which is counter-intuitive at first sight, but when they explain it, it makes sense). My younger brother was recently outraged to be asked, by a woman who appeared to be in full possession of her faculties, which one of us was the older one. 'Him,' he snarled. '*Really?* By how much?' 'Five years.' 'Five YEARS!' If I turn my ears in the direction of Dollis Hill, I can hear his teeth still grinding; for he is much more abstemious in his habits than I am, and even goes to the gym. Or runs about. Or something like that.

It is horribly unfair, and although my estranged wife persists, to this day, in the belief that my slender figure is attributable to nothing more than snorting enormous amounts of cocaine off the firm, glistening bottoms of hookers, it really is down to the combination of a virtuous lifestyle and a speedy metabolism. Well, virtuous is pushing it a bit, as I manage to exceed the government's recommended wine intake by a factor of at least three, have a 95:5 ratio of fatty meat-to-vegetable diet and do little more exercise than jiggling my foot when watching television (although I do have a pair of six-kilo dumbbells which I use, when I can be bothered, for vanity's sake). I think I know what the secret is: it is really down to not being shouted at all day, and being able to get up when I want. And had I been forced to live in some really grisly area like Harlesden, I would have succumbed either to shingles or terminal depression or both.

True, it is not all rosy. A molar cracked in half the other day while I was eating what the copywriters at Waitrose's labelling department had correctly described as a perfectly ripe avocado, and there has been an explosion of mega-zits on the back whose scars I could plausibly pass off as an old shotgun wound ('Anger,' says my friend The Therapist. 'Do you wash your back?' asks Razors). But The Thing I Am Terrified Is Stomach Cancer and The Thing I Am Terrified Is a Stroke and The Thing I Am Terrified Is a Heart Attack have not returned; they used to circle me like malevolent yo-yos. I haven't even had to go to the doctor since being thrown out.

It is, though, early days, and I could well end up like poor Jeffrey Bernard, with enormous goitres on my neck, being pushed around the Groucho in a wheelchair. And they won't even have written a play about me.

*

Meanwhile, the hunt for the next Mrs Lezard continues in its desultory, defeated way. What is it that compels people to seek out a lifelong companion when all previous arrangements have ended in heartbreaking disaster? Talk about the triumph of hope over experience. I have to admit that I do not necessarily represent an enticing prospect. On the plus side I have an enviable Body Mass Index, a good command of cooking, and of French, and almost all my own teeth; but set against that the fact that these days I am compelled to haggle over the price of confectionery in the shop over the road. (Well, I mean, come on. Seventy pence for a Double Decker? They're making it up as they go along.) Once I had a house and a Mercedes (true, a battered one of a hue only startlingly seen in nature that must have knocked about fifteen per cent off its third-hand price, but still a Mercedes); now all I have by the way of material possessions are the laptop I am writing this on, a lovely red guitar, and a bicycle in the hallway with a knackered back brake and two flat tyres. (Offers considered.) I know I was never one to set much store by material possessions, and in fact rather despise those who do, but this is getting ridiculous.

One thinks, inevitably, of Boethius's *Consolatio Philosophiae*, and like him I try to maintain a deep serenity born of the knowledge that one's luck can go down as well as up, but it is the lack of a permanent companion which is beginning to irk me. One of my children asked me recently if I had a girlfriend. 'That's none of your damned business,' I told him, to which he replied, 'Oh, so you don't, then.' Curbing the urge to give him a sound thrashing for his impudence, I said, 'Actually, I've got seven.' That shut him up.

If, though, you accept the codes of Victorian society, where a stolen kiss or the amorous holding of hands pretty much committed you to the relationship, then I suppose I do have something like seven girlfriends. But in the sense of having someone you can regularly curl up and watch films with, go for walks in the park with, etc., and suggest sex to without any serious risk of outraged rejection, then that figure approaches zero. It was not always thus. A woman I will christen the Lacanian and I had a fling last year but it was, to my immense displeasure at the time, decidedly temporary. Apparently the smallest useful unit of temporal measurement is the time it takes a beam of light to cross a proton. It has since been redefined as the length of time the Lacanian thought she was in love with me. I blame myself; for was it not Slavoj Žižek, Lacan's greatest disciple and interpreter, who defined love as 'giving something you don't have – to someone who doesn't want it'? It's not exactly Sinatra singing 'You Make Me Feel So Young', is it? The more I researched Žižek and Lacan to find out what made her tick the more I realised I was in trouble. The irony that I now write for a magazine that tempts potential subscribers with copies of free books by Žižek has not escaped me.

Still, released from the suspended animation of marriage, I have learned, and learned in a hurry, a lot about relationships. Although not going so far as one of my friends, multiply scarred in love accidents, who says that all women should be obliged, like cigarette packets, to bear a prominent government health warning (shouldn't men, too?), I would advise a certain degree of circumspection. You may, for instance, hear a woman say 'Is it too much to ask that I find a man who does not beat me up/keep running off to smoke crack in the loo/sleep with my best friend the minute my back is turned?' I have heard this quite a few times, more times than someone hitherto cocooned in matrimony (married men tend not to receive these cries for help, for some reason), and the company of other couples, gets to hear, and bitter experience has since taught me that saying something along the lines of 'Well, I do none of these things, and I rather fancy you as it happens, how about dinner?' is a waste of breath. Literally. They look right through you. You've got more chance if you say 'Right now, I'm wearing ladies' underwear' – or even perhaps 'Well, it's funny you should mention that, but there's nothing I like more than sneaking off for a crafty rock or two and then beating my girlfriends *like gongs.*'

I have also learned that: 1. you can't make anyone love you back, 2. there's no fool like an old fool, and 3. when a woman says she's mad it is wise to take this assertion at face value and not, as I foolishly did, regard it as a winning and auspicious indication of a mind unclouded by self-deception.

So what now? I have learned to mistrust dating

websites ever since I saw that my estranged wife used the adjectives 'easy-going' and 'tolerant' to describe herself on *Guardian* Soulmates, which, as I sternly reminded her, bore about as much relation to the truth as if I'd said I was 'incredibly tidy' and 'able to fly'.* Thinking Sod This For a Lark, I announced myself on the site as a 'lazy, selfish borderline alcoholic' which actually got quite a few replies, and has resulted in more than one good friendship; but no Mrs Lezard Number 2. There was the woman who looked at the church over the road from the pub and asked me if it was Westminster Abbey, which would have been a surprising question even if she hadn't been a native Londoner (we still snogged later on, but she said, the next day, that there was 'no chemistry', which genuinely baffled me); the woman who wanted to play Rod Stewart's 'Sailing' while we made love, and the woman who asked me to talk to her vagina before I went down on her. (I was unfamiliar with the precise conversational etiquette, and confined myself to phatic remarks about the weather. Well, I was raised as an Englishman.) Ho hum. Does anyone want that bike?

*

---

* I was smarting at the time when I told her this. As it turned out, over time, the qualities she advertised became, happily for all, more evident.

God, as Jesus might have said while dangling painfully from the cross, I hate Easter. Mine has not been so physically agonising as the Redeemer's but it certainly could have done with some improvement. It kicked off beautifully on Thursday night when the bank machine ate my only card. (No credit cards for me. I may be, as my lawyer wrote down in her notes with a sigh, 'financially hopeless', but I'm not *that* hopeless.) The last time this happened was a few months ago, at the same cashpoint. Then, I thought no more about it and went to bed, assuming the card was safe in the machine's innards, but I was called the next day by an anxious bank asking me if I had, by any chance, gone on a wild spending spree among the fleshpots of Leytonstone and Walthamstow (Argos and Asda, mainly). They had detected, in their words, unusual activity in my account, i.e. they had the nous to suspect that not only would I not be seen dead in either Argos, Asda, Leytonstone or Walthamstow, I especially wouldn't be seen dead there early on a Sunday morning.

This time I was prompter about cancelling the card, but not prompt enough to stop the con artists from removing £250 in cash. Platitudinously, inevitably, one's attitude to the people responsible for such acts veers, when it happens to one's own self, from a tolerant liberal-left approach (rehabilitation, education, sympathy) to a more robust policy of slicing their genitals off in public.

OK: so no money. No company, either. The kids are gallivanting on the south coast with their mother and her grateful boyfriend. Razors has pushed off to Canada and then Cuba for three weeks, leaving me entirely to my own devices. This would be bad enough at any time of year but doing so at the beginning of Easter is harsh. Easter is not a festivity that the British do well. Committing to neither the agony of our Lord or the pagan celebration of life, they just scoff a lot of Creme Eggs and shut everything down when the weather is guaranteed to be rubbish.

But you really get a sense of London's failings at Easter. As my old friend John Moore, one-third of the great pop group Black Box Recorder, put it in one of his less cheery solo works, 'I'm tired of London, and tired of life;/I've got to admit it, Dr Johnson was right'. He must have written those words during a bleak London Easter, when the accumulation of what are in effect three Sundays in four days turns the place into something that feels as though it has been hit by a neutron bomb. I'm looking out of the window and I feel like I'm the last man alive. And this, mark you, is in W1. My only company now is a rabble of insubordinate mice, the beautiful girl in Majestic Wine has vanished off the face of the earth, and the telly only plays DVDs. It's like *La Bohème* round here.

It is at times like this that I wonder how London has the cheek to proclaim itself as a city in any honest sense. I remember noting how Vancouver's residents, when I once stayed there, kept going on about how beautiful the surrounding countryside was; but a city, I thought, that defined itself chiefly by its surrounding non-urban aspect may be said to have missed the point of what being a city is all about.

But that's Vancouver, which is at the periphery of the western world, and is occupied by Canadians, who are pleasingly not known for their boastfulness. London, though, has no such excuses. Even when Paris shuts down for August you can find somewhere within walking distance that's open after eleven. (It's about communal human contact, not drink.) Here the only places open after eleven are either Soho members' clubs which charge £8 for a glass of house piss or Australia-themed Gehennas thronged with twenty-year-old Yahoos. A New York friend visited one Sunday shortly after I moved in and suggested we find a nice bar in the area that would be open after ten thirty. Worth a try, I thought. Half an hour later she was screaming at me, and at anyone else depraved enough to be awake at that hour, 'This isn't a city! How dare it call itself a city?' Born and raised here, all I could do was bow my head and apologise.

But it gets worse now. Even Waitrose shuts for the Easter Sunday. It is, indeed, an indicator of my despair that I write a column two days before my deadline, just to have something to do. And in case I simply don't make it through Easter Monday. This is so bad. It's like living in . . . it's like living in the *countryside*.

*

The spring has finally sprung, the sap is rising. The sight of a male pigeon chasing after a female one, his tail feathers brushing the ground, her gait all look-I-really-don't-need-this-right-now, fills me with melancholy. Why this stupid dance of pursuit and flight? Why does the woman simply not say, 'Come and get it, big boy'? I have been on this earth for nearly half a century and yet still never seen the male pigeon do its business successfully. Not that I am sure what such success would look like. I am not at all up on avian biology. What's the deal with eggs? Do birds actually need to have sex? Why didn't little chicks pop out of my breakfast eggs when I was staying at Mr Tom Hodgkinson's place in Devon, the only place I can afford to take the kids on holiday? (These interludes always go well. Their mother asks me to pack their wetsuits and bodyboards because there's nothing my children and I love more than to freeze our tits off in the icy waters off Ilfracombe. The last time I went there I was about seventy miles down the M4 before I remembered I'd forgotten to pack their wetsuits and bodyboards. 'Good,' they said.) There was a cockerel there, and he looked pretty healthy. If this was covered in biology I must have been ill or asleep that week. Come to think of it, biology of all species is a bit of a blind spot for me, and for a long time I used to believe that anal sex was how lawyers were conceived.

A friend sympathetic to my plight emails me. 'Write about boobs,' she advises. 'That way you will actually get to see some boobs.' Hmm. This is obviously kindly meant but I wonder if she has not misunderstood what it is precisely that makes me tick. (For a start, I am more of a legs man. I like to think that, while I am all for boobs, and am happy to wave a flag for them, I have left infancy behind me now, and no longer feel the need to suckle at the tit.) And anyway, what can I say about boobs that has not been said before? Besides, I have better things to think about. A finely turned ankle, for instance. I know a woman who, upon leaving myself and a male friend, said, 'I'll leave you two to talk about women's breasts or whatever it is men talk about when they're together.' We put our heads in our hands. I'll tell you what men talk about when they're alone: we talk about how is it that women think we talk about their breasts the moment their backs are turned? I was about to say the conversation turned to Schopenhauer, but I've just remembered that even he wrote about women's breasts – although in a most unpleasant fashion. You do not believe me? Look it up in his *Aphorisms*.

At least such melancholy as I suffer from is not of a serious kind. Burton would not have included it in his *Anatomy*. It is the type which a friend once described as 'nothing a good bonk, a sunny day, and a satisfying dump can't fix'. (Such a mixture of the sexual and the cloacal will doubtless remind you, automatically, of Earl Butz, Nixon's and then Ford's Secretary of Agriculture, obliged to resign in 1976 when he joked to Pat Boone that all 'the coloureds' – his term – wanted was 'soft shoes, tight pussy, and a warm place to shit'. (The precise order and wording is disputed but this is how I remember it.) This is indeed an offensive generalisation, so serve him right, but I do remember once, when I was getting to the unhappy stage of being married – that stage when even occupying the same room is barely an option, so sex, even cross sex, is right out of the question – sitting in my bathroom through which the winter wind whistled, wearing new boots which were taking an absolute age to break in, and miserably reflecting that I had failed to score on all three counts.)

I am in Regent's Park when I see the pigeons, walking with my friend Amel, who has come from Paris on the spur of the moment. Amel was once my au pair and used to entertain a *tendresse* for me of which I was completely unaware; luckily, nothing came of it, which is why we are still friends. 'The man wants the pursuit,' she says, apropos the pigeons. Being French, this is just the kind of thing she would say, but she is also in the throes of a new relationship. Obviously spring arrived earlier in Paris.

One should be wary, though. Earlier that day I'd been listening to Radio 3 and learned that Frescobaldi's teacher, Luzzasco Luzzaschi, wrote a lyric, '*O dolcezza massimo d'amore*', which warned against the dangers of love: 'love is no friend, don't be fooled by appearances; though he seems gentle, he is sharp and cruel.' The day before Amel had taken me to the Globe to see *Romeo and Juliet*, and it struck me that Luzzaschi was, in this instance, more on the money than Shakespeare in that play, what with all the uplift associated with love; Romeo and Juliet do not stay together nearly long enough to see their love go sour. As I always advise people who are embarking on new relationships, you might be all smoochy now, but mark my words, in twenty years' time you're going to be fighting *like rats in a sack*.

It is, I reflect, a long time since I have been asked to be someone's Best Man.

But it is well that I am not feeling as emotionally labile as I have done in the two years since my separation; otherwise *R & J* would have been unbearable. Instead, I find that my mind, when it wanders, asks: 'What do they do at the Globe when it rains?' and, after seeing another pair of the birds mucking about on the thatch, the old chestnut: 'Why do you never see any baby pigeons?'

*

It will astonish quite a few people who know me, some of them quite well, that I do not actually like scrounging. Unlike my otherwise wonderful great-uncle Lizzie, who was a character in the book *White Mischief* and of whom it was once observed that 'whenever he saw a pretty woman, he would mentally undress her right down to her chequebook', I find it demeaning and humiliating. But sometimes in a person's life one has to modify one's scruples to make ends meet. Scrounging is one viable option, and I would like to pass on a few tips.

It will help your self-esteem to recall that the scrounger has a distinguished literary heritage. One recalls the character in Wodehouse who proudly boasts that he doesn't owe a soul a penny, not counting tradesmen and tailors of course, and the character in Tolstoy who makes a point of frequenting the very establishments where he owes enormous sums of money, just to show that he is not scared, and therefore confident of repaying the debt some time soon. This is a technique which requires some panache to pull off properly, and it did indeed backfire horribly once on me one evening in a well-known London members' club when I made the beginner's mistake of paying my bill with a Maestro card instead of with cash. It set off the alarm which rings when someone who is about a year overdue with their subs is trying to buy a drink and I had what the French, with unusual Gallic understatement, call a *mauvais quart d'heure* as the manager forced me to hand over what was in effect the next month's child support in order to square the books. To settle that matter has involved doing some actual work, which these days isn't the easiest thing to do. There are a lot of jittery and broke writers out there.

As for specific wheezes, one thing I like to do is sit on my own in the Duke at a table which would normally be expected to hold four people eating its excellent but slightly-out-of-my-price-range food. The Guvnor, Alan, who has taken pity on me and yet in some bizarre way sees me as an adornment to his establishment (I helped him get a glowing review in the *Standard*), or at the very least an amusing curiosity, will then shove me over to a less prominent table, but top up my pint by way of compensation. This takes timing, but I've got it down, I would like to think, to a fine art. If some really high fliers come in he will even give me a large whisky just to get me away from them. Poncing off your friends is another matter. Most of mine are in almost the same boat as me, so I can't. My housemate Razors and I scrounge off each other, because even though he earns a fantastic salary, it all goes straight out again to sort out his own tormented domestic issues. He gets paid in the middle of the month, I at the end, so between ourselves we help each other like mountaineers scaling a cliff that would have defeated the solitary climber. And you do find, when you get divorced, that some of your so-called friends never call you again; and some of them lend you £500 when you really need it and say, 'Pay me back when you can.'

Then there is the longer game, such as the one writers occasionally play, called How Long Can I Get Away With Not Finishing My Book? I have strung this one out for a period of time extraordinary even for the most adept and audacious of players. It requires nerves of steel, mind, and you do have to finish the damn thing eventually (I'm working on it! I'm working on it!), but you can get a great lunch out of it every year if you choose the right agent. My own, a man of such wit, charm, and decency that I sometimes wonder if I am not a little in love with him, understands the concept of wining and dining the penniless author. (With my publisher the story is different. Even before he got exasperated to the point of despair, lunch with him was a bowl of noodles and, after repeated requests, a bottle of beer, and the admonition that he was meeting Orhan Pamuk, i.e. a much more important writer than you, later in the afternoon.)

On another note entirely, and to conclude with something which removes us from the sordid realm of finance, I reached another New Low this weekend when I discovered that there were no mussels available from the fish van at the local farmers' market. I had been planning to treat the kids with moules marinières, of which most of them are fond. 'Sorry,' I was told. 'They're not in stock at the moment. It's their breeding season.' Bloody Norah, I thought. Even the molluscs are getting more action than me these days.

*

An ethical poser: meeting Razors and Stefan the ex-barman at the Duke, I ask a couple of young women if they wouldn't mind sharing their table with us (that is: they're already sitting down, and there's nowhere else for us to do so). This is accepted protocol, and, moreover, it is sunny, so everyone wants to sit outside. The women are pretty in that not entirely enticing we-read-every-issue-of-*Vogue* kind of way, and have those big fashionable sunglasses pushed on top of their heads (ladies: it makes you look like you have four eyeballs. Just so you know), and don't look entirely thrilled to be joined by us, but we have no intention of pestering them.

Razors has kindly brought me some Lucky Strikes back from his holiday in Cuba. Manufactured cigarettes are a bit of a treat for me, and I intend to get stuck into them. But as I take the packet out, the woman sitting diagonally opposite says: 'Would you mind not smoking? I get asthma.'

There's a great *Peanuts* cartoon where Snoopy bangs on Charlie Brown's door during a rainstorm. 'Sorry,' says Charlie Brown, 'my mom won't let you in because she doesn't like the smell of wet dog.' There's a silent frame as Snoopy looks indignantly at the door, and then he says to himself: 'My mind reels with sarcastic replies!' Well, my mind reels with sarcastic replies at this point, too.

For a start, we are *en plein air*, which is, these days, the smoker's last fiefdom. We're not allowed inside, you see. There are all these little signs telling us not to. (There are, absurdly, such signs at the entrances to the pedestrian underpass by Baker Street station, and on some of the phone boxes nearby. Strangely, whenever I have broken the law by smoking in them, no one has objected.) Secondly, the idea that outdoor second-hand smoke, with the breeze blowing it away from you, can bring on an asthma attack is ludicrous. I should know: I have asthma too. Thirdly, the women aren't eating or American or anything like that, and fourthly, well, dammit, do I have to go on? This place is my local. You are as likely to find me there as you are in my own living room.

I begin to suspect that the woman is playing the health card not because she really does suffer from asthma, but because she just likes bossing people around. I know it is frightfully ungallant of me to say so, but there is such a type. I am, in fact, intimately familiar with it. Anyway, I decide to meet her on her own ground, and tell her that I, too, suffer from asthma. ('Tell you what,' runs one of my unspoken sarcastic replies, 'I'll suck the smoke into my own lungs and keep it there as long as possible so it doesn't bother you, OK?') The look I receive, though, tells me that she is not exactly on the verge of either embracing me as a fellow sufferer or saying, 'Oh, go on then, I was only messing you about.'

So I say, 'I'll see how long I can hold out for,' which turns out to be about five minutes; I swap places with Stefan so the bossy woman can't see me, and everyone knows that second-hand smoke only offends if the smoker is in your line of vision.

But the episode does give me occasion to reflect on the way this country is heading. There's a Derek and Clive routine where Peter Cook plays the part of a murderously drunk driver having been pulled over by the police, and he says the country is turning, in his vivid phraseology, into 'a Gestapo khazi'. It really does seem to be becoming, literally, that. A vast public urinal monitored by cameras and, where there are no cameras, busybodies. (You see people pissing in the street almost every day, but people are more comfortable complaining to smokers than telling off the public pissers. I saw someone pissing against the front wall of the Catholic church in Lisson Grove the other day. I am as unhappy with organised religion in general and the way the Catholic Church is run in particular as the next man, but even for me, this is a bit much. Yet I did not confront the man.) And the sneak, the informer, is very much officially encouraged by the powers that be. Look at all the confidential hotlines being advertised these days. Premium-rate numbers for benefit claimants; 0800 numbers for reporting alleged frauds. And do people become community police officers, I wonder, because they feel a debt to society, or because they like shoving their noses into other people's business? I imagine it is not entirely the former.

The thing to do is to make a stand. Taking the kids on the pedal boats at Regent's Park the other day with an old friend, we note, on our return, a list of six extremely petty rules, five of which we have broken, and broken extravagantly. By getting our deposit back we seem, technically, to be breaking another one. The children, naturally, are delighted (I couldn't break the no-smoking rule myself, because smoking in front of the children just isn't worth the aggravation, but my companion can do what she likes. And, as I can verify from over a quarter of a century's friendship with her, she usually does). It is important for their authority figure to look as though he is above the law.

Later on, Razors and I have one of those mindless but strangely pleasing Bet-I've-broken-more-laws-than-you-have conversations. I win by a whisker but I don't think I'll be going into details here. You never know who's snooping around.

*

It is funny how relative poverty is. I might have a column in the *Statesman* called 'Down and Out in London', but I'm not really down and out. Well, compared to most of my friends, fellow hacks, and even, I have a hunch, many readers of that noble magazine, I am as poor as a church mouse, as they used to say, but compared to some of the people I see, I am relatively wealthy. I might not be able to afford a holiday (when people ask me where I'm going for mine, my mind reels with sarcastic replies), but at least I have a roof, however contingent, over my head, friends, and can afford to eat.

But the dossers I see every day on my journeys – they're down and out. They're the real deal. I have become attuned to their plight since my expulsion from the family home. It is interesting what happens to one's attitude to the destitute when you realise that you are rather fewer notches on Fortune's game-wheel from the bottom than you were before. You start evaluating others' neediness. You stop saying, 'There but for the grace of God go I' – you start realising that you are two bad phone calls away from having to go back to live at your parents'. And you start giving more.

For not to give to beggars constitutes a very simple and straightforward failure to understand what it means to be human. I am sorry, but when I see someone shivering in a doorway holding out the bottom of a polystyrene cup, the instinct is to put a quid in it.

This is an instinct that can be – and often is, thanks to our powers of self-justification – successfully repressed, but if you're the kind of person who looks at a beggar and thinks 'Why isn't he working?' or 'It's so much better in the long run to have a standing order with Oxfam, beggars only spend the money on drink or drugs' then you are going to have to work hard at becoming a friend of mine. I certainly have my own ways of rationalising, on the hoof, about when I'm going to dish out the alms. There's a homeless hostel round the corner from me, and quite often the inmates either squat outside the Hovel of a morning with their superlagers (perhaps they sense its sympathetic vibrations; there's one couple who, touchingly, do the crossword in the *Mirror* together while they drink), or drop round to the Duke to pester the drinkers outside for money and cigarettes. The last lot who came round were quite a sight. They looked like the most ill-fortuned survivors of some devastating apocalypse. I am almost invariably generous with my snout (a dosser who refuses a hank of tobacco and a few Rizlas is, frankly, taking the piss), but these people had been so depraved by circumstance and cheap cider that they had quite forgotten their manners. Were I a proper Christian, Muslim or Jew this would not have been an issue – I gather the core tenets of these religions consider the giving of alms an unavoidable obligation, with Jesus's nice wrinkle about the left hand not knowing what the right hand doeth being, in my view, a very nice touch (and a precept which, by writing about it, I have failed to live up to). But being an atheist means you can be flexible in your responses and so this time, to the amused but definite rebuke of my friend Z—('You're only a *shaving* away from them!') I said, 'No,' before they'd even finished their sentence. Not good.

But otherwise I do my best. Well, not really, but a bit. I normally fix any chuggers who accost me with a stern and gimlet eye, but not the one from Shelter. That was too close, so to speak, to home. I also buy the *Big Issue* on the same impulse. And there are the regular mendicants. There's the toothless wreck of a woman who, if you look even a little bit closely, has to be under forty but looks a lot older at first sight; the silent man, rather younger, who sits patiently and, unrelentingly, unemployable, the victim perhaps of some great trauma; but then there were the couple, a youngish man and a woman, neither of whom you might want to go on a date with, but who lie together under sodden sleeping bags and newspapers in the underpass by Baker Street station. I give most days to the ruined woman, because she looks as though she's going to die if you don't; the quiet man less often, because he doesn't look quite so wretched, and the couple not at all, because they don't even look as though they're asking for money and also because they seem to have found deep comfort in each other's company. Passing them while they were asleep one night, they looked so touching, like the figures on the Arundel tomb, that I felt like doing something for them – but they looked at peace, self-sufficient, and a lot more at ease in each other's arms than many more affluent couples I could think of.

They've gone. I think of them now, and my failure of charity towards them, because the underpass now stinks, chemically. It always used to stink, chiefly of urine, and enough to make you wonder whether it was worth waiting for the lights to change if you wanted to cross the Marylebone Road; but now the stink is deliberate, unsupportable, designed to force people away. You now only use the tunnel if you're in a real hurry. The question is now settled; the gauntlet of pee and claims on your conscience was far easier to run than this much viler assault on the senses. For this stench is much worse: it's the odour of some eugenicist, at council level, saying, 'Let's make this place stink so bad that not even the homeless can use it.'

*

In what I fear is becoming a recurring motif, times are tight at the Hovel. The relativity of poverty be damned. Because Razors and I are, despite our superficial inclinations towards degeneracy and depravity, reasonably decent and fulfil our obligations to friends and family as soon as we can, we find ourselves in the position of being, to use the sometimes forbidding jargon of the financial specialist, completely screwed. The casual visitor to the Hovel will notice, on top of the washing machine, a small pile of loose change, entirely composed of currency no larger in value than a 20p bit; these are what we fished out of our pockets when we thought, earlier this evening, that we might be able to scrape enough together to buy a bottle of wine. We have enough, it turns out, to buy a carton of condemned orange juice and a jumbo packet of cheese balls, neither of which we are really in the mood for. They would not, we feel, address our despair.

We have, some would say, only ourselves to blame. In my case I blew the last of the month's money (financed by a postdated cheque to the Guvnor of the Duke, it has to be said) on a weekend trip to Cambridge, to entertain (and be entertained by) my fellow miscreant from the boating lake, an old and good friend who is also broke but who would give me the shirt off her back if she could; in Razors' case it was a matter of being obliged, strongly against his will, to pay for a dinner, the details of which it is best to pass over in silence. Let us just say that my weekend was a lot more fun than his.

The funny thing is, this is not credit crunch stuff. When the financial collapse happened and people started whining about, say, having to contemplate the horror of taking their kids out of private school, I found it hard to empathise, if not to sympathise, with their pain, on the grounds that I never, even at the high point of my wealth, could have afforded to put my cat, let alone a child, through private education (nor would I have wanted to – I think it best that cats mix with other cats from all social backgrounds, and do not learn to give themselves airs and graces which prevent them from mixing with less privileged felines who may have just as much to offer in the long run).

No, I've been living in my own credit crunch for some while now. Bring it on, I say. My familiarity with penury may have been as much a function of my indolence and incompetence as prevailing economic circumstances, but it does not invalidate my reflections on economic injustice, which has become more marked and obvious in the last few months. In fact, things have now got so bad I sometimes wonder why there hasn't been some kind of violent revolution.

It is a historical accident that whatever tepid support I have to give to one of the nation's football teams is directed towards Arsenal. This is because when I was seven years old, the school bully promised to flush my head down the toilet unless I endorsed the team for the rest of my life, a deal I readily assented to, on the grounds that they were on line for winning the double at the time, weren't based too far from home, and my head was in the toilet bowl. Yes, why not have Arsenal as a proxy repository for my personal hopes and dreams, I thought. Anyway. Having been moderately pleased at the manager Arsène Wenger's signing of the exciting and talented Russian striker Andrei Arshavin, I was disgusted to discover that he wanted his £80,000 per week salary to be paid as an interest-free loan so that he wouldn't have to worry about the new fifty per cent tax rate.* One has become slightly less inured to the greed and insensitivity of the wealthy footballer than one used to be, but this is taking the biscuit. I could name several friends, writers, teachers, and so on, of incomparable talent, industry and worth, even more broke than I am, who live lives of complete blamelessness; where is their reward on earth? When I talk about socialism to my children, when they need help with their Ancient History homework, I feel like Dr Cornelius, the tutor who, in fear of his life, tells the young Prince Caspian the tales of ancient Narnia.

After a brief discussion of Arshavin's salary, Razors and I went over to the washing machine and looked again at our pathetic pile of cash. We wondered how long it would take Arshavin to earn it. I've done the maths: 0.315 of a second, assuming that our combined worldly wealth amounts to £2.50. I know it's a bit clichéd to use the footballer's salary as a yardstick

---

* Since this was written, as keen football followers will know, Arshavin has since gone on to play like rubbish for Arsenal, to the extent where even the team's own fans have booed him coming on as a substitute, and is at the time of writing on loan to his boyhood club, FC Zenit St Petersburg. I'm not quite up enough on Russian football teams to know if this represents nemesis or not, but shall we just tentatively say that it perhaps serves him right?

of outrage, but there is a reason some things become clichés. It's time to start baying for blood.

*

We have a cleaning lady. You may well ask what a memoir pleading continuous poverty is doing with a cleaning lady, and whether, in fact, it would be more appropriate if she wrote it, but her English is basic, and she comes free with the Hovel and would be cleaning it up whether I was here or not, so what can I do? She's from Romania. She is also good, and honest, and has come, at whatever grievous psychic cost to herself, to understand me. I know a bit about her country's neighbour, Hungary, but bugger-all about Romania, except for the basics about Ceausescu and the fact that relations with the Hungarians are so strained that I think it would be probably for the best if I kept my fondness for the Magyars under wraps *pro tem*. 'I've always wanted to go to Romania,' I said once in order to have some kind of conversation. I hope she didn't pick up the faint strain of mendacity, or desperation, in the remark. Although I once did see some kind of travel programme about the wild forests there and thought it looked sort of romantic, in a Bram Stoker-ish way. But I didn't want to mention Transylvania because she might just think, Another idiot who's only heard of Transylvania because he happens to have heard of

Dracula. 'The Carpathians,' I add, tentatively. Are the Carpathians in Romania? This is awkward.

I am also, I must admit, an incredible slob. Will Self, if I may name-drop here, once tried to teach me how to wipe crumbs and other detritus off a table. 'You don't just dab at the visible stuff,' he said, slowly and clearly. 'You use big, sweeping motions like this.' I looked on uncomprehendingly, like a Neanderthal being shown how to fly a helicopter. (Come to think of it, your average Neanderthal would probably, after a course of lessons, be able to fly a helicopter as well as the next Neanderthal, whereas long and bitter experience has taught me that I am utterly useless at tidying up, and always will be.)

Actually, I can tidy up if a lady is coming round. This can even include the cleaning lady. I have begun to understand the mindset of someone who picks the place up before the help arrives. Once, during a long sex drought, I gave up on cleaning my room. What was the point? This meant that when the cleaning lady came round I'd be too ashamed to let her into the room, so I hid under the duvet until she left. This meant the room became even more squalid. Nothing organic, mind, except for the mould at the bottom of the mugs, and maybe the odd nail clipping; but plenty of papers, receipts, books, oh Lord, so many books, clothes, particularly socks, small change, CDs, cassettes, unmentionable fragments of tissue, little items of office furniture I have no use for, like those tiny bits of green string with metal aglets, there's a good word, look it up, library cards, playing cards for some reason, letters, bank statements, invitations, cards with little bits torn off the edges for roaches, roaches, packaging for various things, empty or partly empty blister packets of Nurofen, band-aids roaming far and free from the comfort of their box, bits and pieces whose provenance and purpose will remain forever an impenetrable mystery, you know, all the normal crap you can expect to pile up around you – only an awful lot of it, and, if you stepped into the room from the normal world, all at once. I now know why I never decorated my post-separation room: it was already decorated. By H. P. Lovecraft.

Eventually, I pulled myself together. I think it was the day I couldn't find my own bed. Or the day after I had to use the completely empty spare room next door for a certain nefarious purpose. Also, the kids were coming the next day, and you don't really want them to think you're going to pieces. It took me about three hours, and it's a small room. Yet I did it, breaking a vicious circle: your self-esteem goes because you've been thrown out of the family home, you let things go a bit, you look at the mess and your self-esteem now exists only at quantum level, you let things go a bit more . . .

These days I am much better. Razors, like all cockney gangsters, is very tidy – they learn it during National Service, I think, or prison – and I do not wish to offend him. He doesn't have to say anything. He just gives me a hurt look, only detectable as reproach by someone who knows him well.

There are still the mice. They were too disgusted to enter my room but they do prance about the place as if they own it. This was endearing when I was lonely and miserable; Mousie was my friend, like Mr Jingles, the mouse in *The Green Mile* who befriends the convicts on death row. But now I'm not lonely and miserable, and they're a nuisance. They once lined up in the living room to watch the telly with us, the cheeky bastards. They poo on the chopping board, as if to say, 'Here's what we think of you and your *fucking* chopping board.'

I catch the cleaning lady looking at the tiny turds.

'Yes, I know,' I say, 'we have a mouse.' She shakes her head.

'You have many mouse,' she corrects me.

'Er yes, ha ha, we need a cat.'

'No,' she says, 'you need more cat.'

I'd be happy with just the one. Unfortunately, the terms of the lease prevent us from having a pet. Although a cat in the Hovel would be an employee, not a pet. Now, what if a stray kitten known to a reader just happened to mislay itself in the Baker Street area, and find its way to a certain house . . . ?

*

As someone who makes part of what we shall for the sake of argument call a living by writing about the trials of the middle-aged man, I like to keep an eye on the competition, for all that this is a crowded field. Leafing through my parents' copy of the *Spectator*, I notice and read a piece by Toby Young bemoaning the lot of the modern father, whom he describes as an unpaid slave to his children rather than anything approaching a meaningful authority figure. Later on, I read Tim Dowling's column in the *Guardian*'s Saturday magazine in which, as is his wont, he describes his own tribulations as a father and husband. For his birthday, his wife has given him a salad spinner.

'Amateurs,' I think to myself. This is not to disparage the quality of their work – Dowling is particularly talented at describing a miserable marriage, and raises the bar very high indeed for car-crash confessional journalism – but to cast an enquiring light onto what they are doing with their lives, or how they are playing the hands that Fate has dealt them. Even allowing for the exaggeration demanded by comic effect, I suspect that Mr Young's authority has certainly been degraded since the days when he was a forceful and commanding editor of the *Modern Review*, under whom, despite our almost completely divergent political views, I was pleased to serve; and I suspect that Mr Dowling has been given, if not exactly a salad spinner, then something not much more exciting or delightful. Although I am prepared to concede that it was, in fact, a salad spinner. My business is not to impugn their veracity. It is to offer advice.

May I respectfully suggest, then, that they get divorced? Drastic, yes, but it would put an end to all the problems they write about. True, it would create a whole new set of exciting and often intractable new problems, but we men like a challenge, on the whole, and it doesn't get much more challenging, outside of the armed forces or the emergency services, than being thrown out of the family home.

My thoughts drift this way as I approach another anniversary of my own ejection from the nest. I know exactly when this is because it is the day after a friend's birthday, which had turned into an impromptu bourbon-tasting session with a couple of mutual friends, both Americans, and therefore very knowledgeable about bourbon indeed. They are also very wealthy, and so think nothing of having a well stocked shelf of first-rate gargle, and pouring loads of it down their friends' throats after closing time.

I will draw a veil over what happened between then and my reappearance at the Family Home around seven thirty the next morning, largely because my memory of that period is a tad sketchy, but it suffices to say that my wife's demand next morning that I find myself somewhere else to live *tout suite* did not exactly come as a bolt from the blue. I recalled the myth that says that all a Muslim man has to do to divorce his wife is say 'I divorce thee' three times; and it occurred to me that this was exactly three times as hard as it is for a western woman in Shepherd's Bush to kick her own husband out.

Since then there has hardly been a dull moment. There have been long periods of deep misery but substantial compensations too. Let us apply them to the two journalists named above. In the case of Mr Young, he will find his position as male authority figure significantly enhanced. Since my own expulsion, after an admittedly rocky start during which I was a ghost of a man, a zombie without appetite, I have eventually found relations with my children improved beyond measure. Instead of the bipolar skivvy who kept shouting at them to stop bothering him, they now see a fearless Byronic exile, genuinely delighted in their company for every second he has it. The delight is mutual; and there is no one around to undermine such charisma as I possess by drawing attention, in tones of high contempt, to my habit of, variously, twiddling my fork when I speak at the dinner table/letting my trousers get hitched up over the back of my Chelsea boots/being too short. (I particularly resented this last one. It is not as if I had been dissembling about my height for the previous nineteen years.) True, these trivia were aired as a means of not bringing up rather more serious derelictions, but being told I was a twerp in front of the children forty times a day did not, I think, enhance their respect for me. That's changed.

As for Mr Dowling, it all rather depends on whether he is actually telling his readers the truth when he writes about his own family life. Let us, for the sake of argument, assume that he is. For those not familiar with his work, he regularly describes a domestic regime which combines ritualised psychological warfare with the deprivations of the Gulag. His wife, let us not put too fine a point on this, does not come out of his bulletins very well. A salad spinner, indeed. Even my own soon-to-be-ex-wife, at the very nadir of our relationship, i.e. being barely able to sit in the same room as each other for two years, always came through with the goods on my birthday – rather better than I did on hers, if truth be told (but this is a problem common to most men. I said we like a challenge, but within reason, you know?). I suspect that Dowling's column may very well in fact be part of an ongoing campaign to be given his own marching orders – it is easier to play the wronged party if it happens that way round, as opposed to stomping off oneself.

It will, of course, be hard at first – so hard, in fact, as to not seem worth the bother. The first six to eight months will, as I have said, be spent more or less entirely in tears, or, if they are going to be stiff-upper-lipped about it, on the verge of them. Any artistic representation of domestic unity – e.g. *Family Guy* – will be unendurable. (I know that the gorgeous Lois's eternal devotion to her oafish and obese husband is itself one of the programme's ongoing jokes, but it still hurts to see it.) The only music they will be able to listen to will either predate or postdate their relationships. They will be broke. But in the end – consider the freedom, the recovery of self-esteem. I'm amazed people don't do it more often.

*

In news that will have pretty much the same devastating effect on my female readership as Paul McCartney's marriage to Linda Eastman had on millions of Beatles fans, I have to say that the search for the next (in effect) Mrs Lezard has come to a shuddering but very welcome halt. No further applications for the post will be accepted, but I would like to thank all those who put themselves forward. Standards were consistently high, especially when you consider my own gruesome looks.

Still, one can always find flies in the ointment without even bothering to look. For a start, the fine weather might mean that you can take a beautiful woman punting without freezing to death, but back in London it means there is the depressing inevitability of redundant advice on public transport, in which we are told to carry a bottle of water with us at all times. Never mind the redundancy; you get the feeling that a population which has to be reminded to avoid thirst in hot weather has reached such a level of stupidity that maybe a natural cull of the dimmer elements might be in the interests of the gene pool.

On a more personal level, I had a very *mauvais quart d'heure* last week when I got a phone call from the Child Support Agency. What made matters worse was that, as I was driving, I asked my son to answer the phone. 'Who is it?' I asked. Like many children, he becomes tongue-tied and nervous on the phone, and I had to repeat the question many times, with increasing volume and impatience, so the CSA got to hear me shouting, 'Jesus Christ, WHO IS IT?' which must have made a marvellous impression. 'Hmm, not only stingy but abusive too. And takes the name of the Redeemer in vain.'

The Guvnor of the Duke sympathised with me in his usual fashion. 'The CSA? What's that, a posh ASBO?' Precisely. He then advised his staff not to give me further credit until the matter had been resolved.

Luckily, the matter has been resolved. Thanks to my usual technique of bluster, idle threats, and humiliating climbdown, the ex, increasingly easy-going and tolerant, called off the hounds, for which I am happy to express public gratitude. You do not want the CSA after you. They are as humourless, inflexible, and relentless as the Spanish Inquisition. (And, in this instance, quite as unexpected.) They tend not to see the bigger picture, and do not look indulgently on one's consumption of wine, even though I was once told by a doctor not to stop, because my system would go into shock.

The only other fly in the ointment, apart from the continuous penury (for reasons which should not take too much thought to work out, I entertain a reverie of spotting the ex-editor of the *Independent on Sunday*, the one who rang me up saying 'I've been looking at the figures . . .' and deciding that having his very own radio critic was about to sink his paper for good, as he begs for small change by Baker Street station, and kicking him up the arse) is in fact a wasp, which stung me on the knuckle as I picnicked with the person I shall henceforth refer to as the Woman I Love. As I write, every stroke of the keyboard to the right of the Y is accompanied by a howl of agony. It could have been worse: a few years ago I got stung on the eyelid and the next day, when I looked in the mirror, I saw William Leith, in one of his podgier phases, staring back at me. (This is not to speak ill of the admirable Mr Leith's looks. It's just that they're his, not mine, and I was unaccustomed to seeing them in the glass.)

The only even vaguely interesting thing about being stung on the hand, apart from making me recollect the Schmidt Sting Pain Index (a yellowjacket sting rates only 2 out of a possible 4 and is described as 'hot, smoky, almost irreverent', like 'W. C. Fields stubbing a cigar out on your tongue', which seems a trifle understated to me), was that this was the one to which I had moved my wedding rings, items of little monetary and (now) even less sentimental value. (They just look nice and I like fiddling with them in non-smoking environments.) But I had to shift them quickly before they started cutting into the quickly swelling flesh. But where the hell was I going to put them? It dawned on me that the best place for them was where they had been originally – on the ring finger of the left hand. In other words, I was going to have to go around looking as though I was married again – only without the hunched and defeated manner of those who are unhappily so. Most men neither bother to look, or care once they have, whether women are wearing wedding rings or not, but, believe me, women do notice these things. So as I am happily off the market they may as well stay there.

2

It is about midnight on a Saturday. I am lying full length on the decaying garden bench on the back terrace of the Hovel, having a cigarette and brooding on life, and the party that is taking place across the way. There is a very *Rear Window*-ish aspect to the rear of the Hovel, which is great, as it would be rather exciting to discover a murder taking place on the other side of the courtyard, particularly if you were with Grace Kelly.

No murders tonight, though; but a very loud party. It sounds like fun. There is a lot of whooping and from what I can tell there are more girls than boys there. At which point one of them leans out of the window and calls out 'Oi! Come on over!'

Well, why not? I appear to live in a part of town where impromptu invitations are handed out on a regular basis. I recall the time when I was entertaining a couple of friends on the terrace and a man leaned out of a window a couple of floors up and a house to the left. Instead of asking us to shut the hell up he asked if he could join us. After conferring – were there enough of us to overpower him if he turned out to be a loony? – we asked him if he could bring anything, and he brought down a bottle of Grey Goose and a gramme of coke. He *did* turn

61

out to be a loony, though. You do not have that many tattoos, or muscles that big – his upper arms were about the size of my thighs – or disappear forever the next day leaving your BlackBerry behind if you are a merchant banker, even if your name is Javier. (I tried to give it back to him but he wasn't having it. I kept it for a year, not using it and a little worried that if I recharged it I'd find many increasingly vexed messages from the Medellín cartel; I finally gave it to my daughter upon the next but one completion of her losing-her-phone cycle.)

When I trickle over to the party a few minutes later, I am struck by a number of things. The first is, golly, what a lot of drunk girls there are. They are doing that thing of dancing with each other whereby Girl A grinds her bum into the crotch of Girl B, while Boys A, B, C and D's eyes pop out on stalks. Everyone there is about thirty, and so, to my eyes, looks incredibly youthful and healthy. I, on the other hand, feel like the Ancient Mariner, only not so garrulous. 'Do you dance?' one of the girls asks me. She may as well have asked if I fly space rockets, or play the Theremin. I do not dance. Women have fallen out of love with me when they have seen me try.

But the others, who do not know this, are looking at me with friendly curiosity. Perhaps I seem frightfully exotic to them. And they must be pissed enough not to find my age and looks actively repellent. Something like an orderly queue for me forms. In fact, I haven't had this much attention from women at a party since . . . well, ever. As luck would have it, I am very happily spoken for, as I explained earlier, and so completely off the market that my only impulse is to flee. I find out that it is indeed a thirtieth birthday party, and that most of the people work for Rio Tinto.

'Ah,' I say, 'I used to demonstrate against you.' (Anyone else here remember Rio Tinto Zinc? They were Very Bad, for some reason.)

My interlocutor drifts off and I try and work out what else is wrong with this picture. The place is very clean. It doesn't look like one o'clock in the morning. I remember from the mid-1980s a place off Fitzjohn's Avenue where a party had been going on for months; no one had ever got round to stopping it, and the house was so large, and so multiply tenanted, that a kind of twenty-four-hour shift pattern evolved; while one bunch recuperated, another lot took their place. And as everyone was so out of their minds on drugs few people could tell or care if it was day or night. Now *that* was my idea of a party. (I drive up Fitzjohn's Avenue every couple of weeks or so to see my folks and sometimes wonder, wistfully, if it's still going on.)

But at this party no one is even *smoking*. At which point I realise the appalling gulf that exists between myself and the younger generation. They're drinking some vile concoction involving Coca-Cola and – ??

– mint leaves? – that not even I can finish. They're nice enough people though, considering they're all probably filthy rich and have never read a book in their lives (a nosey stroll through the place reveals no evidence to suggest that I'm wrong).

I grow old, I murmur as I return home, I grow old, I shall wear the bottoms of my trousers rolled. Who now knows Eliot, or has his lines etched into the brain? Well, I suppose these youngsters' forebears from twenty-odd years ago, as they watched, baffled, hordes of grungy students waving placards denouncing what was then Rio Tinto Zinc wouldn't have known any Eliot either. Every year, the clever people competing on *University Challenge* fail to indentify an image of T. S. Eliot. I have become used to this. And it is not as if knowing a few snatches of modernist poetry has brought me great wealth or bovine peace of mind.

I look around me at the Hovel, so dilapidated in comparison with the place I have been in that it seems not far off attaining the status of a condemned building. And yet it stands. Its wiring has been checked, and if it looks shabby on the outside, it has Character. This is much more like it, I think.

*

Sunday, 6 p.m.: to the pub quiz at the Uxbridge Arms in Notting Hill. A funny time for a pub quiz, you might think, but it used to suit me down to the ground. It was, when I was married, more or less the only time I was allowed out of the home, even though, as my wife never failed to remind me, it fell smack in the middle of feeding-children-and-putting-them-to-bed-time. Oh really? How unfortunate, I would say, although this, I have to say, constituted one of its chief attractions. But I felt that as I had done a lot of the feeding-children-and-putting-them-to-bed stuff for the previous six days of the week, I deserved an evening off.

Now that I no longer have the impetus of flight from the family home to shoot me into the pub, it must follow that these days I only go there for the pleasure of it. Which, as I type those words, somehow does not strike me as quite the right way of putting it.

It is not like other pub quizzes. There is a fluctuating but generally stable hard core of about a dozen regulars, and we mingle among each other to form teams of, depending how many people are there, between two and four. The main objective among teams is not to be saddled with S——,* a very nice lady who parts company with reality on or around her third glass of Pinot Grigio, and E——, who is best described, unfortunately, as a cantankerous old

---

* As you can see, I am going to refrain from naming names in order to spare some blushes.

****. (He goes to India a lot, in order, as far as I can gather, to let the local Hindus know that they have not, in fact, reincarnated to a higher plane of existence, and that there is still plenty of suffering for them out there. When one of his visits coincided with the terrorist outrage in Mumbai of 2008, reaction in the Uxbridge was, shall we say, robust. 'Jesus,' said J— the rich American, 'you pay all that money and they still can't get rid of one little old guy.') Everyone puts two pounds into a half-pint mug; the winning team pockets what is left after the second-placed team, and the quizmaster, have been bought drinks. Winning the pub quiz, then, can leave you seriously out of pocket. The idea is for the knowledgeable not to get above themselves.

Newcomers and innocent bystanders are encouraged into, no, shamed or bullied into, taking part: the young are particularly welcome, for they cannot pace their drinking, not that it would matter much if they could, for they know absolutely fuck-all about anything, especially when the quiz is set by the regulars, none of whom are ever going to see forty-five again, and whose frame of reference reflects this.

However, such solidarity as exists among the regulars is, at best, superficial. The real point of the quiz, as far as I can see, is not to win, but for everyone to shout at each other. The casual observer may be forgiven for thinking that he has stumbled into a riot on a Saga holiday. (That was one of the questions once:

what do the letters 'Saga' in such a context stand for? No one admitted to knowing.) See that word in asterisks on the preceding page? That one gets used a lot. Even the landlady gets into the spirit of the occasion. She can make the famously rude Norman Balon look as delicate as a courtier at Versailles. Once she had to go down to the gents to slap some Dulux on a peeling door. 'Hello, Linda,' said M——. 'Got the painters in?' 'No, I'm always like this,' she snapped.

As for the questions, the general idea is not to make them too obscure, but it is only the impossible ones that stick in the memory and can be recalled for the purposes of invective. Personally, I don't see what's so hard about the question from the first quiz I set – 'List the following fielding positions in clockwise order, starting at twelve o'clock from a right-handed batsman's point of view: gulley, mid-off, midwicket, point, mid-on', but I get stick about it four years down the line; similarly, I do not think T——'s friendship-threatening extravaganza, when he played the intros to ten power ballads on his laptop and asked us to identify them, is going to fade from outraged memory for a decade.

The best thing about the Ux quiz is that it represents an atypical cross-section of British society. (I was going to qualify this with the proviso that lack of worldly success is a common theme, but then I remembered that James Lever, author of the Booker-longlisted *Me Cheeta*, sometimes shows up.)

M— used to operate cranes but is now a minicab driver; E— the cantankerous old **** is a plasterer, T— is a sommelier, and I've forgotten what the rest do, if I ever knew, but you won't see them pulling up to the pub in brand new Porsches. Tell you what – why don't you turn up yourself next Sunday? You'll learn some new swear words, and we could always do with your money.

*

It is another exciting evening on the back terrace of the Hovel. I am exiled from the forward-facing parts of the house because the Thai restaurant over the road, following a power failure, has been supplied with a very noisy generator by the electricity company, EDF, who seem content to let the damned thing run for a week without actually sending any men in to solve the problem. (Thinking that this is good for at least a free meal for two – it is not the best restaurant in the world, but it is, as far as Razors and I are concerned, the nearest restaurant in the world, and so receives our patronage whenever we feel flush – I walk in one lunchtime and ask to see the manager, in the hope that he can perform the act of empathy which will enable him to comprehend how hard it is to go to sleep with a generator twenty yards from your ear. The waitress, in what turns out to be the closest we ever get to real communication, hands me a menu.)

Anyway, back to the terrace. The weather, thankfully, is warm and dry enough to stay out with the laptop. It is, again, midnight, and over the slightly muffled noise of the generator I am catching up with *Torchwood*. I then hear an almighty noise coming from an unfamiliar direction. It sounds like a small but well laden lorry has fallen on its side on the other side of the house. I idly wonder whether to investigate but the menacing aliens in *Torchwood* have demanded ten per cent of the world's children and I wonder how long it will be before a cabinet minister suggests this might be a good way of ridding this nation in particular of its underachievers. (Not long, as it turns out. 'What are league tables for?' is the excellent way the question is put, or answered.) I am gripped.

Just then a voice comes from behind me and to the left. 'Excuse me, sir.' In nearly two years at the Hovel no voice has ever come from over there, let alone one addressing me as 'sir'. I am surprised at the way I don't have a heart attack. 'Excuse me, sir, but have you seen anyone come this way? We're police officers.'

Police officers! I say no, but that I did hear a noise which might have come from the roof.

'Have you got a torch?'

Funny thing, a police officer going about his business in the middle of the night without a torch, but I refrain from saying so. Instead I volunteer to check the skylight and make sure that no vile miscreant is trying to murder Razors in his sleep and make away with our priceless collection of half-empty cereal packets. All seems secure.

'So what's going on?' I ask. When the Old Bill are trying to catch villains I like to be public-spirited.

'There's a brothel here. Quite common,' he adds with unnecessary sarcasm, 'in W1.'

'Are you closing it down?' I ask.

'Yes, that is the general idea.'

My heart sinks. There are two incompatible attitudes to brothels. One takes the view of the wit and dandy Sebastian Horsley that sex is the most beautiful experience that money can buy (look his stuff up on YouTube if you are so inclined); the other is less forgiving. It would appear that PC Plod takes the latter view. From the judge's summing-up at the trial of Paul Pennyfeather for white slave-trading in *Decline and Fall*: 'For these human vampires who prey upon the degradation of their species, society has reserved the right of ruthless suppression.' For my part, I am just depressed that there has been a brothel operating right under my nose, or just round the corner from it, and I knew nothing about it. Leaving the rights and wrongs of prostitution aside for the moment, I think it adds a certain louche tone to an area to have a knocking-shop in the vicinity, especially if clients and employees are both discreet enough to keep their existence a secret for years. My friend L— used to be a very vocal enthusiast for prostitution. He kept recommending I go to one establishment in Marble Arch, where the girls were beautiful, the prices far from extortionate, and they gave you a beer if you asked for one. I mumbled something about exploitation and human trafficking, and he said, 'Bollocks. These girls are all saving up for psychology degrees, sending money back home and are still making a packet. Well, more than you at least. And they're smarter than you. Which I suppose isn't saying much in either case.' I never went. I wonder what has happened to L——.

I also wonder about the noise I heard earlier. I would imagine, of all indignities, to be caught in a raid on a house of ill repute to be right up there with the best. There is a certain timeless hilarity about it, if one considers the position vis-à-vis the embarrassed punter. It is, I presume, not as amusing to contemplate the women working there. Was the noise I heard that of some terrified Lithuanian girl in her scanties knocking over a chimney-pot? Or, rather more excitingly, is some respectable MP or judge, seeking to relieve himself from the cares of office, now hobbled by his trousers round his ankles, contemplating in raw panic the collapse of his career as he scampers along the rooftops of Marylebone? I will never know, but whoever it is, I wish them luck. Up to a point.

*

A word with a lawyer. We are talking divorce, and, among other things, arrangements for childcare.

'The point is that you have to have a place which can accommodate your children which is not too far removed, in comfort and amenities, from the home they're growing up in with their mother.'

This, it occurs to me, is a tall order. How many divorced men live in quarters as spacious as the ones they have been obliged to desert? Inevitably, my thoughts drift towards the Hovel. Location, say the estate agents, is all, but there are other aspects of a home.

When I first entered the Hovel it immediately struck me that here was a place that was not for responsible, modern homeowning adults. The bed of a grown-up householder projects into the middle of the room, so that it can be approached from each side; students, prisoners, monks and children all have beds jammed against the wall, so that they can only be entered in one direction. It is so in the Hovel. And no one could mistake the Hovel for a child-friendly environment. It certainly falls down, in comparison with the family home, in terms of number of rooms, size of rooms, number of pianos, number of pussy cats, number of gardens, number of floors which do not slope at fifteen degrees out of the horizontal,* and number of bathrooms where the lights actually work.

---

* I know, I said ten earlier. It seems to be getting worse.

This last is the latest in a line of entropic events which characterise the domestic these days. Remember: we are all in the unshakable grip of the second law of thermodynamics, which means, basically, that everything falls to bits, and the bits never reassemble themselves in any useful way. They just flop about uselessly, like guests at the ragged end of a party too smashed even to move or speak coherently. There was the time when the telly suddenly stopped working; Razors and I, mystified as to the cause, which seemed to come from beyond the telly, took this stoically, as men do, and so did nothing about it except look at static for a couple of months. 'Fixed the telly yet?' he would ask on his return from work. 'No,' I would reply, and this Beckettian dialogue went on for some time, even when children would come and also, in their rather more strident way, ask if anyone had fixed the telly yet. In the end we discovered that there was simply no aerial on the roof. This rather baffled the TV repairman, until we worked out that a previous tenant had been mooching the signals off the neighbour's rig, and when he changed his system, he disconnected us.

The bathroom light is another matter, though. This had always made a disconcerting fizzing noise when on but I thought little about it; electricity *should* make a fizzing noise, like in old Frankenstein films. When the light stopped working but the fizzing noise continued I thought I'd better investigate. Unscrewing the globular ceiling lampshade, I discovered it was full – quite full – of water. I wondered to myself how much, on a scale of one to ten, a lightbulb socket entirely immersed in water counted as a health and safety hazard. Ten? Eleven? The latest theory is that it is due to the decayed grouting in the upstairs shower, which allows excess splashy water to run down through the body of the house (the downstairs bathroom is unusable *qua* bathroom, in that the bath itself has a leak it would take the entire rebuilding of the Hovel, or the Deathtrap as I am now tempted to call it, to fix. But you can still use the sink).

So now, in short, I have to take my contact lenses out in the kitchen; there is a mirror propped up by the chopping board for this very purpose. New visitors to the Hovel see this mirror in its unusual place and assume that this is an indicator of druggy decadence; they raise their eyebrows suggestively, but are gently disabused. It's odd, though, how taking contact lenses out in the kitchen is much more problematic than doing the same in a bathroom. I've now lost three left contact lenses in as many weeks ('Why?' I cry to an unhearing God, 'and why only the left ones?'), which is playing havoc with my supply of monthlies – I discovered, some while ago, that the monthly contact lens is a con, even worse than the sell-by date on a jar of honey; I managed to keep using the same pair of monthlies for five years. I thought I had enough to keep me going until the year 2020, but for want of a bit of grouting all my plans are dust.

But back to the children. As it turns out, they have come to love the Hovel, and look on it as a combination of pirate's lair and funhouse. Indeed, what with the removal, at some point in the 1960s, of a supporting beam, many people comment on the similarity of the Hovel to the crazily tilted house in the Bosco dei Mostri in Bomarzo. You haven't seen it? Next time you're in Lazio, you absolutely must. If you can't afford the flight to Italy, just pop round here. If you dare.

*

Enormous changes at the Hovel. We have a toaster. Quite how I have managed to live for nearly two years without a toaster escapes me; how I have managed to not only maintain my Body Mass Index, but actually put on weight, without a toaster, beats me completely. Depression and solitude, I found, made me lose all interest in cooking, which was itself a cause for further depression, as, if I say so myself, I have a reputation as quite a good cook, my South-east Asian crispy duck stuffed with an incredible but tasty array of exotic spices having been considered worthy of inclusion in the local primary school's book of worldwide recipes. (I was once, though, so hungover that I made a chilli con carne while forgetting to put in any onions, which, as I realised, was like writing an article and forgetting to put in any nouns; but even that wasn't as bad as you might have thought, and my guests were very nice about it.)

But we don't entertain at the Hovel, at least not in a dinner-party way, unless we're having a toast party, which we have never been confident of doing, particularly as we have a rather poor track record when it comes to putting bread under the grill and taking it out before it gets horribly burned. It is after the latest in a long series of toast-related catastrophes that I cry 'Enough!' and go to John Lewis, taking the Woman I Love with me to stop me from buying a Dualit toaster (which cost hundreds of pounds *and still burn your toast*).

Our mission accomplished (and what a strangely moving experience it is, looking through the electrical goods section of John Lewis, for all the world like a young couple contemplating their wedding list), we return to the Hovel, our hearts pounding with excitement. The good and conscientious people of John Lewis have thoughtfully provided an instruction manual for their own-brand two-slice toaster. Razors and I pore over it carefully. You might think that operating a toaster is like riding a bicycle, in that once mastered, the skill never leaves one, or that a company which decides to go into such details about this not-exactly-arcane method of food preparation could be said to have scant faith in the intelligence of its customers, but these days you cannot be too careful.

'Place one or two slices of bread in the bread slots,

and press the handle right down until it latches.' This is straightforward enough, or would be, were it not for the ambiguity contained in the words 'one or two'. Which is it to be, we ask? One, or two? We need help here. There are actually three of us at the time – Razors, myself, and the WIL. In the end, out of sheer giddy euphoria, we decide to go for the full two slices, bearing in mind that 'If the toast starts to smoke before it has popped up, toasting can be stopped by pressing the Cancel button'. Not to mention the wise words 'If you should find that the toast is not dark enough you may wish to toast the bread again.' (Then again, you may not. You may think, 'Screw this for a game of soldiers,' and eat slightly undercooked toast. But the instruction manual, perhaps mindful of the delicate sensibilities of John Lewis's customers, which is nice of them, considering that if they're all like us then they're the kind of cheapskates who don't want to spend more than £10 on a toaster, omits this.)

The adventure is not over. We dimly remember that there is more to this toasting lark than just putting the bread in the slots and pushing the handle down. Luckily, here is the manual to help us: 'When toasting has finished, the handle will rapidly rise to the fully raised position.' They're not kidding. Boiing! Up it leaps, like a salmon. 'The toasted bread can now be removed and the toaster is ready to recommence toasting.' You mean, we ask ourselves with a wild surmise, we can do this again? We can, and do, gorging ourselves on toast until we are sick at the very sight of it.

But my heart goes out to the poor sap who had to write the instruction manual for the toaster. One can imagine the scene. John Lewis's in-house copywriter, whom I see as a young man crushed by a year's unemployment following a decent 2:1 in English, has been asked to supply instructions for a machine that even a baby intuitively knows how to operate. The job, not in itself the most richly fulfilling that he can imagine, has suddenly got worse. He can see where it will all end, as, with half his mind elsewhere, he taps out his weary phrases on his Mac. Some smart Alec taking the piss out of him in a national magazine. To which I can only say: Don't worry, mate. I've been there, too. It gets better eventually. Sort of.

*

It's holiday time again. Having invented the staycation – no, I don't like the word either – nine years ago when we ran out of money and out of patience with French traffic, we are sticking to principle and hanging out at Tom Hodgkinson's gaff in north Devon. It's always fun, especially looking after the fauna: pony, cats, chickens, bees and now ferrets, which are like draught-excluders with legs and are the devil to catch.

One problem is that the place we are staying in has

its own microclimate, whose significant characteristic can be summed up by the word 'rain'. I know it is a trope from which all comedy was finally extracted about fifty years ago, but the rain-lashed British holiday is something my brood and I are getting to be quite expert at. (How well I remember the sodden family holidays in Cornwall, where every year, after a pre-motorway nine-hour drive, we'd watch my father stomping round a launderette, whose windows were steamed up, it seemed, by his own fury, saying the words 'never again' like a mantra. Happy days.) So perhaps I shouldn't be so surprised at how well (relatively) a twelve- and a nine-year-old boy can behave when confined indoors with only one parent – but, really, I am.

Some years ago I used to write a column for the *Guardian* called 'Slack Dad' (the phrase is mine but has since been pinched by other, more shameless columnists), the premise of which, as you might be able to work out for yourself, was a very hands-off approach to fatherhood. Miraculously, it seems to have worked. I know there are few things more rebarbative than parents who insist, usually against all the evidence, that their children are the bees' knees, but something seems to have turned out fine with mine. All right, it's not all rosy in the garden. The youngest, whose likeness you will find against the word 'contrary' in all good illustrated dictionaries, has been winding us up all summer by announcing that he is supporting Australia in the Ashes. This has placed me in a painful predicament, as I believe that an Englishman has no higher purpose in life than to make an Australian cricket fan miserable.

But the atmosphere has largely been wonderful. This is not in any way to cast aspersions on her, but family holidays under identical conditions with Mrs Lezard used to be more testing occasions. There is, and I need not be sexist about this, a certain kind of family authority figure who is not happy unless the family unit is Doing Something. Holidays become a nightmarish inversion of the ideal. You know, the concept of the vacation as a period in which one relaxes. Instead there were excursions. A trip to the beach would become so stressful that I wonder if it didn't take as many years off my life as smoking forty untipped fags a day for forty years. And have you noticed how much less packing a motherless family generates? In the old days, the car, by no means small, would be so crammed with luggage and whatnot that the rear-view mirror became a useless frippery. Nowadays it's three small bags, a road map, a cricket bat, a couple of balls, a bag of sandwiches, a tube of fruit gums and a bottle of water, and we're off. This time we even had space to bring along the eldest's guitar and amplifier. We could have fitted in a pool table had we so wished, but Tom's gaff comes with one already. (In a spidery and quarter-derelict barn, spattered here and there with bat shit, but it is level and does the job.)

It is funny how one acclimatises oneself to the situation. I used to see them the way we used to see lepers, the separated fathers with their children, eating their joyless, anxious meals at Pizza Express (I have a hunch that, were divorce made illegal, Pizza Express would probably go under). Their misery seemed palpable, contagious, a place of terror and retribution. Fly straight, I would say to myself, or you will end up like that, ruefully contemplating the days of security and happiness. One would also worry as much about the effect on the children as on oneself. Not only will one have to stump up for university fees when they are older, there will be endless psychiatrists' sessions to pay for. (You can't expect your offspring to pay for them if they're your own fault, can you?)

But, as I said, the children are giving every indication of being well adjusted. OK, so there's the one who supports the Aussies even when given the opportunity, around teatime on the fourth day of the Oval Test, to become an Englishman again. It is, I suppose, a heavy price to pay; but there are, it has to be admitted, heavier ones.

*

I am lunching at the Duke with my good friend the Moose, aka Kevin Jackson, the noted wit, polymath, raconteur, pataphysicist and vampirologist. I am trying to wangle a part in the promotional film for his new book, *Bite*, to which I have been looking forward for ages. I volunteer to be First Corpse. There will be no fee but the prestige of being associated with such a project will be worth more than rubies. 'Nick Lezard – First Corpse', he writes in his big notebook. 'What's my motivation?' I ask. 'You're dead,' he says.

The Guvnor comes and joins us. He is looking even shiftier than usual, which tends to mean he is going to play some practical joke or mind-game on me. But as he is generously subsidising our lunch I know I will have to go along with it. The Guvnor has, shall we say, unusual business contacts. The day before he had been flown to Le Touquet for lunch. Why don't I get flown to Le Touquet for lunch? Ever? And what's he doing going to Le Touquet anyway? He's a fucking pub landlord, for goodness' sake. Today he hands me a packet which advertises itself as a herbal libido and performance enhancer for men, given to him by the manufacturer, who was a guest at the Duke earlier. 'They used to call it Herbal Viagra,' says the Guvnor, 'but Viagra got the hump.' I begin to feel that sensation so familiar to me when I enter into conversation with the Guvnor, that I am in an unusually rude, postmodern episode of *Minder*. He tears off a couple of pills from the packet and hands them to me. They are large, and brown. The Guvnor suggests, to put it somewhat more delicately than he did, that I try them out on my own and report back to him. I assure him that not only do I have no problems in that particular area, but I have to do some work that afternoon. 'Well, let me know how you get on anyway,' he says.

A couple of days later I am with a certain lady who, having had this run past her, decides she does not wish to be named even pseudonymously, but frankly you don't have to be a rocket scientist to work out who she is. We have had a nice dinner, a few glasses of wine, and are feeling perfectly happy and mellow. I pull out the pills and explain their provenance. I add that although, of course, I have no problems in that particular area, it might be fun to have a go with them and see what happens, how about it?

Wisely, I had taken the precaution of jotting down the ingredients off the box when at the Duke, and we looked the main ones up on the web. The days in which I put any old rubbish into my system in the pursuit of pleasure are long gone. No side effects are mentioned, so I take them. 'For best results do not take after food,' said one website, so I imagine I won't be getting the full benefit. This doesn't bother me for, as I would like to assure my readers, I have no problems in that particular area.

Now, I have always been slightly sceptical about the assertions of herbal practitioners. From now on, though, such an attitude is undergoing fundamental revision. On the matter of the basic claims made by the manufacturers, let us simply say that they are justified. But there is more. Before hustling the aforementioned lady up the stairs with some urgency, I begin to feel a slightly psychoactive effect, as of a very mild tab of E. The next couple of hours we shall pass over in silence, except to say that if I ever had a problem in that particular area before, which I did not, I certainly don't now; indeed, I was told that there was marked improvement on what had previously been considered perfectly adequate. The bad stuff comes later. Sleep proves fitful in the extreme. Such sleep as I manage is haunted by dreams of extraordinary vividness and dread. In one, I dreamed I was, I promise you, trying to buy a pipe while being menaced by panthers. Analyse that one, Dr Freud. The next morning I feel dreadful. My eyes are bloodshot, and sensitive to light. My hands tremble. My ears buzz. I resemble nothing so much as a Victorian poster-boy advertising the perils of fornication, particularly as I am still walking around with what is, for all intents and purposes, a bowsprit. There is only one part of my body that is not unwell, and I want it to go away. I have, in short, a very pressing problem in that particular area. (I text the Guvnor to complain. His reply: 'They work best on people with small cocks.' Cheers, Guv.)

It took a day for that problem to go away; two days for the bad dreams to go away; four days for me to recover my health to an even modest approximation of what it was once. Boys and girls: these pills mean business. Leave them alone. Unless, that is, you want to play a corpse in the Moose's film. How they get the coffin lid to stay down is someone else's problem.

*

'What a drag it is getting old,' sang Mick Jagger in 'Mother's Little Helper' when he was about twelve years old, the insensitive bastard. Well, he's wrong. I reflect on my age as I pass the time by filling in some stupid online survey by National Rail (don't get me started) and discovering that I am now in the penultimate age bracket before you have to tick the '60–dead' box.

Ageing has its unforeseen benefits. When I was much younger indeed, I used to be amused by an American book of my parents' called *Flipsville – Squaresville* (by Stan and Jan Berenstain, in case you're interested) which humorously listed the differences between parents and teenagers. One half of the book was intended to mock teenagers; you turned it over and the other half did the same for adults. Just as one of the defining moments in the ageing process comes when you realise that you have more sympathy for the parents than the daughter in the Beatles' 'She's Leaving Home' (running off with a man from the motor trade? The hussy); or that when you watch an old episode of *Fawlty Towers* you find yourself monitoring the first disconcerting stirrings of desire for Prunella Scales as Sybil Fawlty (while at the same time, paradoxically, *completely* understanding where Basil Fawlty is coming from), I now find that what was meant to be risible in adults is actually rather pleasurable.

For example, one of the things that teenagers noticed about adults was the way they would just sit around 'making all kinds of dopey noises'. This observation was accompanied by a not unfunny drawing of a middle-aged couple sitting in armchairs going 'hmm', 'wee', 'pfft', etc.

Now, sitting around making all kinds of dopey noises is something I happen to be getting rather good at. And now that I am living with a man the same age as me, this habit is, I fear, getting out of control. Making dopey noises for no really good reason at all was about number 36 in the list of reasons why my wife wanted to get rid of me (if I lop off the first twenty-five reasons, then I can consider myself unjustly used), and even my children started to complain about it, but living with someone who has reached the same point in the *cammin di sua vita* as I have, it is as if some kind of competition between us is going on. Listen to us from the other side of the door, and wonder what it is we are doing that could elicit such groans, such gasps and turbid exhalations. Are we trying to lift a sofa unaided? Vividly recalling, with profound shame, a disgraceful episode from the night before? Wondering what it is in our lives we have done wrong, or failed to do? Ejaculating into Beyoncé Knowles? No; we are sitting down. You should hear me when I'm pulling off my Chelsea boots. You'd think there was a lion in the room, and I was wrestling with it.

And talking of Beyoncé Knowles, you should hear the noise Razors makes when he sees an attractive woman on the television. A low, subterranean, sustained Neanderthal growl, which seems to come from the very pit of his being. I am reminded of Malcolm Muggeridge's remark that the greatest thing about old age was the end of sexual desire, living with which had been like being tethered to a wild animal. Well, that wild animal is now very much alive, living in the Hovel with me, and particularly audible when the woman who reads the London news on the BBC comes on. (As for his reaction to the weather girl on the Gaelic channel, I think it best to draw a veil over that.)

For the old, left to their own devices, and without the restraining hand of example and simple good manners to restrain them, take great pleasure in these outbursts. They constitute, in fact, one of life's great pleasures for those of us with scant financial resources and a lot of time on our hands. For we have reached that awkward time in life, Razors and I, when we are too young to go bouncing around shamelessly like Janet Street-Porter, and too old to be automatically considered as potential objects of desire by random strangers. Razors told me how mortified he was when he went to a nightclub once and was approached by a pretty girl. Wahey, he said to himself, I still Have It. The girl then asked, 'Are you the minicab?' When he said he wasn't, she then asked if he had any drugs. Cab driver or drug dealer; these, apparently, were the only circumstances that would account for his presence. And the punchline to that story is that it happened a good fifteen years ago. (I got banned from nightclubs some time before that by my wife. Reason number 17 – and therefore a legitimate one: I can't, and must never again attempt to, dance.)

So, sitting around making dopey noises it is, then. May I also recommend saying 'tsk' from time to time? It's a very satisfying noise of disapproval, and is what 'Mrs Brady – Old Lady' says in the comic magazine *Viz*. Actually, she's not looking so bad these days.

*

A trip to Paris with the Woman I Love. This is my first trip abroad for over two years, and I am so excited I don't even mind having to get up at 4 a.m., which seems to be the only time one can take advantage of the cheap Eurostar deal. I will spare you the details of our stay except to say that Paris is the same as ever, only more crowded with tourists and shockingly expensive. I had also hitherto assumed that the Euro and the pound had not yet achieved parity but once you've been rooked for commission you will find that £100 will get you about €90, which in turn will get you two gin and tonics and a croque-monsieur with no tip. We are managing to avoid the expense of a hotel thanks to the incredible generosity of my friend Amel, my ex-au pair who has since – I am so proud! – become a teacher at the Sorbonne; yet even with a free gaff Paris sucks money out of us like a Dyson. At one point, as I contemplate, on the verge of tears, some mind-boggling bill, I wonder whether I am going to have to become, like George Orwell, a *plongeur* in a restaurant, sleeping in some vermin-infested fleapit. *Down and Out in Paris and London* is not, by the way, a good book to read before a trip to Paris. You read sentences like 'It is a mere statement of fact to say that a French cook will spit in the soup – that is, if he is not going to drink it himself.' I do not order any soup while there but at one point I dice with death by ordering a steak tartare, which leaves me feeling uncomfortable for a couple of days.

But leaving all that aside, the return to London is miserable, and not just because it involves a temporary separation from the WIL. I start up a big angry debate on Facebook when I ask people to tell me one way in which London is superior to Paris. Apart from taxis, which don't count because you can get by without them in Paris, the only half-convincing example is given by my friend Louisa, who says

London is better 'because it's got us in it', but that's not really Paris's fault. Everything is better in Paris. Atmosphere, food, sex, light, walking down the street holding hands. The warnings on cigarette packets tell us that *fumer peut entraîner une mort lente et douloureuse*, and yes, I do know what that means, but it still sounds like it's a line from Baudelaire (it's almost an Alexandrine). You think better in Paris. I lost count of the number of bookshops I came across. You sometimes even get the impression there are more English language bookshops there than there are here. I particularly recommend the incredibly browsable Abbey bookshop in the rue de la Parcheminerie, 5th arrondissement, where, after a boozy al fresco lunch, the owner refused to accept payment for a copy of *The Unquiet Grave*, itself a hugely francophilic book and one which contains much that is useful and wise ('women differ from men in that to break with the past and mangle their mate in the process fulfills a dark need', etc. I wonder: what on earth made me latch on to that particular aperçu?).

Back in the Hovel, there are momentous changes. We now have another occupant – a woman. Razors and I have got into a pleasant blokey routine of an evening – like Fureux, the Communist drunk in *Down and Out in Paris and London*, Razors likes to throw empty wine bottles around when he's had a few – but now that there is a feminine element to the Hovel we are learning to behave. I am certainly having to rethink my formerly somewhat laissez-faire policy on walking around the place during the day in my underpants. This woman is in fact my good friend K——, down on her luck yet still one of the nicest and wittiest people I know, so having her around is a pleasure but I suspect she does not appreciate our happy-go-lucky approach to domestic hygiene. Razors says he saw her cleaning the tops of the doors the other day. 'Doors have tops?' I asked. One evening I come home and feel a displacement, a sense of airiness, vacancy, a realignment of the Hovel's geometry. I eventually work it out: the enormous pile of review copies (a dozen books a week minimum for two years, imagine that), about as large and menacing as an unstable Welsh dresser, has been tidied away. It is not as if they have been thrown away, either. It is as if, in a benign version of H. P. Lovecraft's alien topologies, she has found an extra dimension, a pleat in time and space, in which they can be stored. How does she do it? I am amazed, and, I must admit, a bit self-reproachful. Maybe I can learn something.

*

Well, that was quick. K—— has decided that, on balance, the place is not for her. She stayed, in total, about four or five nights; the rest was spent with friends in the country. Whether this is down to her own painful circumstances or is a reaction to male tolerance of squalor I do not know, for we have not discussed the matter, but Razors and I are feeling culpable, and sheepish. We have done guilt-makingly well out of it – she's left us, *pro tem.*, a flatscreen telly – well, flatter than the one we used to have – some stylish dining chairs and a globe which opens up and becomes a sort of drinks trolley – but we feel we have failed a test.

For there are differences between men and women. To think that there was a time when it was orthodoxy to claim that there were none! There's a nice line in Victoria Coren's excellent book about poker which, addressing this matter, points out that women do not take a pint of milk out of the fridge, sniff it, make a face, and then put it back in. But men do. When I read that it was as if someone had switched on a light. How often, I asked myself, had I done that? And why? Answers, respectively: countless, and I haven't the foggiest, unless it is something to do with a reluctance to make life difficult for oneself in the short term. And who knows? Maybe it'll smell better tomorrow. Or one's standards will change, or time's arrow will reverse. Anything beats sorting it out.

Actually, the Hovel isn't too disgusting these days. Or not as it was. When I first arrived there was an Australian computer guy called Greg living here who had an extremely laid-back approach to washing up; Razors tells me that the system used to be for the plates to pile up in the sink for a week, and then for the cleaning lady to take care of them on Fridays. That's no longer the case. Leaving the washing up for the cleaning lady leaves her less time to be horrified and depressed by the state of my room.

(Of course, I have to qualify that 'isn't too disgusting these days' – the place is actually a shambles at the moment, because I write on a Monday, the day after the fortnightly visit from the kids. I can't quite believe how much chaos three children aged between nine and fourteen can cause, particularly when you don't have a dishwasher. You don't notice it so much when you live full-time with them, because it's continuous and all around you, but when they only turn up on alternate weekends, you really see the difference. That's something no one warned me about as being one of the side effects of marital disaster.)

But we had been looking forward to K——'s tenancy precisely because she was a woman, and therefore different, and therefore able to supply us with a different perspective on things. There are times when the Hovel gets a little testosterone-heavy for my liking, and when I catch myself laughing at a quip by Jeremy Clarkson on *Top Gear* I realise that I am going down a slope with a very murky destination at the bottom.

I prefer the company of women to that of men, as a rule; for one thing they're more interesting to talk to, as long as you keep them off fashion. (Even then you can get some very good advice, such as if you are going to buy a Crombie overcoat, it must fit perfectly.) But they're really good at giving advice on how to deal with other women. Such advice as is given is never the same from two different people (basically, it's either along the lines of 'bombard her with letters' or 'don't make any contact for at least THREE DAYS') and so could be said to be of debatable or even risky utility – the thing is, they love being asked for advice about their sex by men, precisely, I suspect, because (a) they love casting judgement and (b) it is their pet topic. It's like meeting a nuclear physicist at a party – a nuclear physicist who really, really likes nuclear physics, not one of those nuclear physicists who's not really into it and wishes he'd been a driving instructor or a cheesemonger instead – and expressing a more than mild or polite interest in nuclear physics, and a wish to know more. You will get to hear stuff, at fascinating length, about nuclear physics you would never have imagined, and you never know when the knowledge will come in handy.

Anyway, K—, come back whenever you like. Living in the Hovel is like being a Ring-bearer: even the briefest exposure, like Sam Gamgee's, marks one for ever. You are among a select group of people. You'll always be welcome. Whether you want to come back or not is another matter.

*

God dammit, another hole in my shoe. Remember that bit in the film where Withnail complains that he's nearly thirty and the sole's flapping off his shoe? Well, imagine being nearly *fifty* and having to face a hole in the very upper leather of the Chelsea boot; the kind of shoe trauma that cannot be mended by the cobbler.

So it has come to this. I have reached that point in my life when I look at the Reader Offer in the *Guardian* for two pairs of mail-order shoes for £60 and go, 'Hmm, not bad, if only I had £60,' instead of saying, 'What kind of pitiable wretch would buy items of clothing, even such intimate ones as shoes, from a newspaper advert, even if that newspaper is one he writes for and has been reading devotedly since the age of five?'

But I think I am going to have to bite the bullet. We are approaching the time of year when a whole lot of bills are coming due, and clothing wears out, so economies have to be made. And let's face it, it's not as if I'm the world's pickiest dresser. I may have had my column adorned by a full-length photo showing me wearing an Aquascutum jacket but I got it for £15 in the local Sue Ryder shop. And the only suit I have that actually fits me, i.e. the only one I've bought in the last ten years, came from John Lewis, and was paid for, humiliatingly, by my mother. (When I told her how much it cost, she replied, 'Too cheap.')

This, I realise, is becoming part of a pattern. In the

past, I could rely on women to clothe me. One gave me a gorgeous and very well-made woollen jumper a couple of years ago, which I suppose I had better get round to washing; last year, when the previous Chelsea boots gave up the ghost, another bought me another pair, a kindness that almost made me weep, for winter was coming on, I had even less money than I do now, which is saying something, and the only other shoes I had were a pair of mouldy, flimsy desert boots which had been bought from a shop on the Uxbridge Road the previous decade for £14.95. Last year another bought me my first pair of Converse (I gather this is the correct plural of 'Converse') since childhood, even though that has prompted some people to murmur 'mutton dressed as lamb'. That woman was in fact particularly keen on grooming me, and her fashion tips have on the whole been good, or at least they were last year, with the exception of her advice that I wear my hair long, which, after a point, made me look like Martin Amis's (imaginary, I stress) older evil brother.

So I wonder if there are any other couture hints I can pass on to the middle-aged man on a budget which do not actually involve theft.

Well, the first is, obviously, the generosity of women. They do tend to be good at this kind of thing, although alarm bells should start going off when they try and make you change your look too much. It bespeaks an underlying dissatisfaction with the way you fundamentally *are*, and I don't just mean in your dress sense. But let us leave aside that question for now. I know that this reliance on their kindness has its own circular, self-defeating logic, which I will dignify with the name Lezard's Paradox: if you are in such a fix that you need the woman in your life to buy you clothes, there will be no woman in your life to buy you clothes. (I have been extremely fortunate to dodge this conundrum in the past, I know.) Failing that, there is the charity shop, where one can choose from a wide range of beige fur-trimmed velour jackets with lapels the size of Herefordshire, inappropriate flared pinstripe trousers which smell of wee, jumpers festooned with pom-poms like tennis balls, and dress shirts which Roger Moore in his pomp would have rejected for being too ornamental. If you are lucky you will find a decent white shirt for a tenner, but I snapped up the last of those, from the Cancer Research shop on Marylebone High Street, last month. And then spilled red wine on it. Readers, if you have anything that will fit a five-foot-nine-inches tall gentleman of slim build, you may send it to me care of Faber and Faber, Bloomsbury House, 74–77 Great Russell Street, London WC1B 3DA. Nothing too gaudy, please, and natural fabrics only.

3

To the dentist. First with my eldest son, who has been complaining of pains which are like toothache but are not exactly toothache. This sounds frustratingly vague but when he complains about something hurting him, we take notice, for he is quite an astonishingly stoic boy. When picking up even the more extravagant grazes and knocks of active childhood, he just says quietly, through gritted teeth, little more than 'Ow'. I, though, have only to *hear* about these injuries to go into a sick faint.

It turns out the boy only has a gum infection (although as I have discovered, and am to be reminded later, these can still be excruciating), so on the walk back to Baker Street station I text his mother, who has asked for news: 'M— is having his front two teeth taken out without anaesthetic and frankly he's being a bit of a wimp about it.' (M— and I giggle together as I compose it.) His mother, though, fails to spot that this is a joke and texts back in a bit of a flap, so I have to call and reassure her. 'Oh,' she says. 'I've just shown your text to my friends here so they can see how insensitive you can be.' I ask her to put them right, but whether she does or not is something I suppose I will never know. I think she will, though, and, besides, it is nice to be able to laugh together for once.

But back to the dentist. The alert reader will have gathered that he practises somewhere near Baker Street. And that alert reader would be right. For my dentist is in Wimpole Street, and – get this – he's NHS. I flung myself at him in about 1986, just before the iron door clanged down forever on people who wished to avail themselves of state-subsidised dental treatment. That he also practises in the traditional part of town appeals, I am afraid, to the social, small-c conservative in me. He is, as all good dentists should be, Jewish. That is, I think he's Jewish – he's got a Jewish name, he's got a Jewish inflection to his speech, and he is, after all, a dentist, but I don't think he's ever affirmed his heritage to me. But if he's not Jewish I'll eat my hat.

And another good thing about him: he's a socialist. Over the years, as I have sat twitching and flinching as he scrapes away the accumulated plaque, I have heard him denounce a succession of health ministers: Kenneth Clarke, William Waldegrave, Virginia Bottomley, Frank Dobson, Alan Milburn have all withered beneath his informed and passionate scorn. (I never heard what he had to say about Stephen Dorrell, for during his two-year stint as Secretary of State for Health I simply forgot to go to the dentist, as the feckless boulevardier often does.)

Anyway, while I am there with my boy, he reminds me that I failed to turn up for my six-monthly check-up and scrape. There is a cancellation at 11.15 on Thursday.

I am reluctant to go, for I have been hiding from him. Grief and despair can take physical form, and in my case this meant I took it in the mouth: gums became infected; a back molar split in two under the horrendous pressure of a MacDonald's cheeseburger (which was disgusting, but only 99p)*. He fixed the back molar by screwing something tooth-like into the gap; that came out after a fortnight. He said there was hardly enough of the tooth left to fix anything on it. The replacement gave up in unequal struggle with a Milky Way after a week, and since then I have learned to live with the shard of tooth, which even after nearly a year still feels weird to the probing tongue. And besides, although I love my dentist more than many would consider possible or even seemly, I felt we had been seeing rather too much of each other lately, and people might start talking.

So, as I sit back in the familiar chair, I say I have a confession to make. (I have already made one on the form they handed me in the waiting room. They are updating their records, and among other things want to know how much I drink. I write 'Lots'.) He is going to find out in about five seconds, so I tell him about the shard. I expect mild rebuke – he is not a fan of my drinking and smoking – but he delivers none.

---

* This being the same tooth that collapsed in the Ripe Avocado incident mentioned on p.23; the cheeseburger completed the job the avocado began.

Indeed, even if he has anything to say about Andy Burnham, the current Secretary of State for Health, he is keeping it to himself. No, he says, resigned to entropy's victory, there's no point in trying to fix it. And it comes as a kind of relief to discover that there is something about me that is, officially, beyond repair.

*

To my brother's for dinner. He rang up on Hallowe'en and I had nothing on. Razors is away, the Duke is unendurable, being full of braying businessmen having early mass corporate Christmas dinners (my God, the noise! The people! How can they make such a racket, and how can they imagine that anything they say is worth hearing?), the Hovel is not the kind of place which attracts trick-or-treaters, which I suppose isn't such a bad thing really, and earlier in the day, reading a book review in the *Guardian*, I learned that according to John T. Cacioppo and William Patrick, 'loneliness harms cognitive functioning, the immune system, and even the expression of DNA in cells'. Being lonely, and having no wish to compromise my immune system any more than I already do, harm such cognitive functioning as remains to me, or repress my cells' ability to express their DNA, I decide to go along.

Which means the situation must be desperate: for

the brother's home, though very nice, was the first place where I resided after the expulsion from the family home, and so, through no fault of its own, has become associated with the most miserable period of my life. These associations are powerful. As it happens, I am now going through a period of equally intense misery, so, what the hell? Why not go back to a place where I know how to be miserable?

I very nearly bail out when I discover that there is no Jubilee Line for the weekend – indeed, half the Underground network seems to have gone bye-byes. Why did this kind of thing not happen in my youth? This cessation of services would have been just the ticket then. I used to have to go to school on a Saturday, which I think is one of the things which has fucked me up for good but has at least left me with a passionate hatred of private education. I remember shivering and cursing at seven thirty in the morning on the outdoor platform of East Finchley, my only consolation being the fact that I could light up inside a warm, comfy tube carriage on the way. I could also toast myself under the fierce heat of disapproval from the other passengers – you can collect some really filthy looks if you smoke while wearing a school uniform, even when you are of legal age to do so. (I had a great anti-smoking moment the other day. Ambling along to Waitrose, I unconsciously fell into step with a sour-faced middle-aged woman. 'I crossed the road to get away from your cigarette smoke,' she snapped.

'And now you're following me.' Reader, be proud of me; I held my peace. I did not say anything along the lines of 'Well, I'm going to have to cross the road to get away from your sanctimoniousness,' or make some ungallant Groucho Marx-esque remark on the unlikelihood of anyone ever wanting to follow her, unless it was for some kind of bet. Instead I just rolled my eyes and walked to the other side of the road again.)

But the new idea that weekends are times for the tubes to take it easy for a while is most unwelcome. One of the great things about the tube – possibly its greatest thing – is that it is not a bus, it does not get stuck in traffic, sandwiched for twenty minutes between a removal lorry and an inconsiderate oaf driving a Range Rover. Do you know how long it takes to get from Baker Street to Dollis Hill on a Rail Replacement Bus Service? About as long as it takes the average sinner to get out of Purgatory, with the added proviso that your post-Purgatory destination is, if the authorities are to be trusted, a lot nicer than Dollis Hill, especially on a dark, dank October evening – you know, that time of year when you know the sunlight has gone out of your life for the foreseeable future. Still, it is nice that they don't actually charge passengers to use these buses – which themselves, as you'll know if you've used one yourself, have a shifty, provisional air about them, as if they've been naughty buses in a past life and are now in disgrace, not allowed to have a proper number again until they have expiated their sins. (Hm. The purgatorial note again. What's all that about?)

So these buses wind their tortuous way through the darkness, and sometimes the driver gets the name of the tube station he's stopping at correct, and sometimes he doesn't, and London gets shittier and shittier, and the people on the bus don't look right, either – they're all people who wanted to avoid getting on a bus in the first place – and I have a sneaking feeling that if my brother and his lovely wife did not live in Dollis Hill, then I would probably never go to Dollis Hill of my own free will. But then again, I don't want my own sadness stinking up the Hovel. I mean, I have to live there.

*

An invitation to the countryside from C——. She has heard things are not going well for me, even by my standards. She's actually an ex from university days but has become a good friend again even if she reads the *Daily Mail*. (I suppose it cuts both ways. Someone recently described me as 'a jolly nice chap even though he writes for the *Guardian*'.) She lives in the village of Kersey, acknowledged by Betjeman – or was it Pevsner? – to be one of England's prettiest, and indeed it is gorgeous; it is also, if you believe this kind of thing, held to be one of England's most haunted, and was the scene of one particularly spooky event in the 1950s, when three naval cadets on leave there underwent what was later described as a 'time slip' – they suddenly seemed to step back six hundred years into the past, finding themselves in the village as it would have been in the times around the Black Death. Later interviews with an initially sceptical historian corroborated, or at any rate compounded, the veracity of their story.

Certainly Kersey can have a disorienting effect on the effete urban visitor, and although C— 's company is always a delight, I have to think twice before accepting her invitations. For country life is not like city life. It really actually is a bit like *The Archers* – but during those periods when the scriptwriters of that programme have a collective rush of blood to the head, decide that now is the time to pick up the pace a bit, get some new listeners in, and with a bit of luck make the news. I have been sworn to secrecy about some of the shenanigans over there but life was never dull. Among the friends I have made there are Heroin Nick (who has, I am glad to have gathered, since kicked the habit, but the nickname endures) and Tom the Burglar (whose burgling days, I am glad to have gathered, are long since over, but the nickname endures), who might not have been the most conventionally respectable of village residents, but were far and away the most amusing. (The conventionally respectable residents are largely of comparatively little interest whatsoever, with the possible exception of one or two others, but let's not drag them into this hall of infamy.)

However, 'amusing' can also mean 'trouble', and in the hothouse atmosphere of a small village with only one pub, a limited supply of available women, and a seemingly unlimited supply of simmering feuds, tempers can get a little frayed, emotions stretched to the point where they twang, pool cues wielded to the point where they snap. I have at times returned from Kersey all but sobbing with gratitude to be back in London, where people observe the proprieties and behave with impeccable civility to each other. Because I am actually dropped into the real maelstrom of village society, and not operating as a tourist who thinks he's getting in with the locals because he's staying in a room above the pub, trips to Kersey can make me feel like one of the terrorised dupes of a Saki short story – 'The Unrest-Cure', perhaps; although it should be admitted that Kersey did have its cultured side. Once, I knocked on the novelist Peter Vansittart's door, on the off chance that he'd be in and willing to receive me (I'd reviewed his *In Memory of England* favourably about ten years before) – which he did, charmingly, in dressing gown and slippers, offering us a choice of either Scotch or sherry at ten in the morning, which, for a man nearing his nineties, was pretty classy, I thought. Sadly, he died not long afterwards.

So three factors have to be taken into consideration when being given an invitation there. One: how psychically robust am I feeling? Two: how much work do I have on? And three: how pissed off will C— be if I blow her out again? Unfortunately, although the answer to the third question is 'quite a bit', the answers to the first two are 'not very' and 'loads'. Which is a pity, as it is my current fragility which prompted the kind invitation in the first place. Also, Razors is poorly – because he doesn't know how to look after himself like I do, he's been coughing his guts up for weeks now – and needs to be cared for.

So even though the weather is lovely, I have to stay in London. I begin to wonder if I will ever get out of here again. I mean, let's face it – am I hard enough?

*

The sun is shining as I write, but I have learned not to trust it. As soon as I step outside, it will start raining. This generally seems to have been the pattern of things for the last couple of years. Indeed, if there were only one piece of advice I could give the separated man exiled from the family home, it would be 'Always carry an umbrella, because for some reason it is going to start raining on you a hell of a lot more than it used to'.

> *Westron wind, when wilt thou blow?*
> *That the small rain down can rain.*

> *Christ, that my love were in my arms,*
> *And I in my bed again.*

Not that that is quite right – the poet would appear to be yearning for rain, only just not too much of it. Perhaps another quatrain is better:

> *The rain it raineth every day*
> *Upon the just and unjust feller*
> *But mainly on the just, because*
> *The unjust has the just's umbrella.*

I did for some time have a particularly fine umbrella which I had, I must confess, stolen myself, or, shall we say, picked up inadvertently. Normally the most honest of people, a kind of giddy amorality seizes me when I attend a function somewhere terribly posh which I know I won't be going back to again. (I do hope the Norwegian* Embassy doesn't do an inventory of its ashtrays at any point in the near future.) The umbrella came, I think, from some newspaper do in one of the Pall Mall clubs, and was elegantly and classically simple; black, with a fine wooden handle and a surprisingly well designed ferrule. (Lovely word, ferrule. I remember my old friend Jeremy Scott telling how he had been shrieked at by

---

* The nationality of the embassy has been changed to protect the guilty, i.e. me.

a schoolmaster – this must have been in the '50s – when he confessed to having caught a dose off some local girl: 'You have put your person where I would not have put the ferrule of my umbrella!' Guess which public school he was at at the time.) It looked so classic in design that it could have been made at any time between 1900 and 1940, but was not ostentatious. Normally having a dismal track record when it comes to keeping umbrellas – if they were dogs, I would now be restrained by court order from keeping one – I held on to this one through thick and thin.

Unfortunately, umbrellas, like love affairs, do not last forever however much you'd like them to, and after one particularly blustery day I was left waiting in the school playground for my youngest underneath a small triangle of tattered, flapping fabric, the bared spokes of the brolly splayed crazily over my drenched head, while small children cavorted around me as if I were, for all the world, like a silent film comedian suddenly made flesh. At least I had the consolation that I was making them laugh. The trick is to maintain a Buster Keaton-esque immobility of expression.

So now I have to rely on the fold-up umbrella. This is too big to go in a pocket and the handle is too tight to fit on one's arm. Nothing ever goes right on this excrescence of a planet. Still, it is at least reasonably well made (cf. those free umbrellas which sometimes used to be given away with the *Evening Standard* and which disintegrated if you sneezed while holding them; still, a nice idea in theory, and probably one of the most English things a visitor to the city could expect to see in half a lifetime), and even though it does not have one of those spring-loaded mechanisms which mean you can make it open at the touch of a button, it is, for my nine-year-old, pleasingly reminiscent of the dimensions of a sawn-off shotgun, though how he worked that out I would rather not speculate.

In the meantime, I wonder if there were not some kind of metaphysical umbrella one could employ to ward off the worst effects of the vicissitudes of life that seem to come thicker and faster at one as the years progress. Oh wait, there is one – it's made in the McLaren Vale district of Australia, and is available for £6.99 from Majestic Wine Warehouses, down to £4.99 if you buy more than two. Which I think I will.*

*

A nasty letter from Her Majesty's Revenue and Customs. By 'nasty' I mean pant-shittingly terrifying: a £20 per day fine until I sort myself out. (I am hazy on the details of what 'sort myself out' might entail;

---

* Since this was written, these prices have, thanks to a combination of the gruesome cupidity of the Australian wine industry, and the strength of the Australian dollar, more or less doubled. My favoured analgesic these days comes from Chile, although it is the same colour.

not, I suspect, that they use such a phrase. I do not know, actually, what kind of a phrase they use at all: I have to get Razors to open their buff envelopes and give me the gist of the contents while I curl up behind the sofa in the foetal position, making faint mewing noises.) Anyway, it needed but this. How they can draw extra water from a well which is already dry seems to have become, all of a sudden, my problem rather than theirs. My policy had always been that if I didn't bother them they wouldn't bother me but this seems to have backfired. There was an advertising campaign they used to try to encourage the self-employed to fill in their tax returns: I vaguely recall an avuncular city gent reminiscent of the *Evening Standard*'s Bristow who was meant to inject a little friendliness into the business but didn't fool anyone, and he wouldn't be impressed or amused by the two or three plastic bags full of receipts which are the only fragments I seem to have shored against my ruins.

The snag is that I really have a big problem filling in my own tax returns, or even adding up my income and my expenses and sending them off to an accountant. For a few years I thrashed around every few months with a shoe-box of receipts and a medium-sized hardback book from Ryman's but eventually even this got too much for me and I rather pathetically got my wife to do it for me. If at any point I have been harsh about this woman let the record state that she knuckled under with this irksome task for years without exacting anything unreasonable in return, and I will be forever grateful for this period of respite. But it goes without saying that this service has stopped for good. I know a woman who would sew on her husband's trouser buttons even after he'd kicked her out but doing the estranged spouse's tax returns is a step too far, even I can see that.

This is the nub, then: I am really bad at this kind of thing. In so many other areas I am more than competent. I can cook, speak a few European languages with varying degrees of skill, fix a broken-down car or motorbike far more often than you might imagine, and am generally a good person to have around in a crisis (although I have had an unfair amount of experience of crises, having been implicated at the root of so many). My children still love me, I can tune a violin, a ukelele and a guitar, and I have the grudging respect of some of my peers. But when it comes to organising, in even the most rudimentary way, my finances, I am what my father would call an Absolute Shower. I have asked around among my friends – few of whom, as you might expect, are likely to win the Tax Form Filler-In of the Year Award – and I have only found one who is more incompetent than me; and she already pays most of her tax via PAYE so I'm not sure that counts. (And do people still say PAYE? Is that not a reference that dates me as much as the Home Service, *Top of the Pops*, or democratic socialism?) The only explanation I can think of is that at some point around 1992 I had a stroke which left me with all my faculties intact, save that of the ability to do my books. Can I claim some kind of medical exemption? (Even when a HMRC-appointed bailiff came round a few months ago, he decided that he was being faced with someone who was sinning more from incompetence and idiocy than a deliberate desire to withhold money from the Exchequer, and didn't bother me since. But I have at least learned never to answer the doorbell before nine in the morning.)

This has been the low, rumbling thunder in the background which has provided the chief darkness to my adult life, but as Shakespeare puts it, so foul a sky clears not without a storm, and here it comes. Should I declare the truckle of cheese and the £20 note mailed to the Duke by my most loyal fan, or the red shirt sent to me by a reader from France? 'A red shirt does something for a man,' she writes in her accompanying letter. 'I'm not sure what, though.' It seems to have brought me luck, both good and bad, very quickly, and she says she only spent one Euro on it – but am I going to have to tear it in two and send one half to the taxman? Or do they want the whole shirt off my back? It really is all I have to offer.

*

Illness strikes. I think it is because I have had the jab for swine flu: and I reflect that one of my bitterly favourite words is 'iatrogenic'; that is, an adverse reaction caused by medical treatment. (One of my more amusing friends tells me that what I really have is wine flu. Oh, how droll.)

Not that I am one to complain. For a start, the chief symptom of whatever this lurgy might be is that it leaves me incapable of doing much more than lying in bed all day reading books, and as that is what I do most of the time anyway you could say that no real harm is being done. There is also a strong disinclination to write, though, which is more problematic, as that is how the money comes in. (Would that there were some way of earning money by reading *and doing nothing else*; to be paid just for the purity of my reactions.) But I am surrounded by kindness, which is funny, because that is the subject of the book I have to review this week. It is very good, and thought-provoking, although rather heavy on the psychoanalysis. 'In Freud's community of solitary, desiring individuals attached "in the first instance" to their instincts, kindness is a bribe. Kindness is foreplay.' Razors comes into my room and expresses sympathy. Would I like a cup of tea and some toast with Marmite? This is very kind. Unusually kind for Razors. Is there a glint in his eye? I know he is a man of strong passions and deep, primal needs. Has he looked at my firm, taut buttocks one too many times and decided to try a bit of Strange?

No: he's just being nice. I have heard, though, of

the kind of marriage where the woman regards the man's illness as itself morally reprehensible, beyond kindness because it is somehow, obviously, his fault. Not having been in any kind of marriage for some time now, and also not even very ill either, Razors' humane act almost reduces me to tears.

But being unwell – even at this low level – does give me pause for thought. What, I wonder, would happen if something went seriously wrong? In the marital home, where one is never left in peace for longer than five minutes outside school and office hours, one's corpse would be discovered long before it would have started to putrefy. In the Hovel, this would not apply if Razors was off on one of his jaunts abroad. Reading Hardy's *The Well-Beloved*, which is in some respects a dreadful book (you can see why after writing it he finally, after some pointed suggestions from reviewers that he do so, gave up fiction and turned to poetry), I note how the sculptor Jocelyn Pierston, when old and ill, and having suffered a string of rather silly love affairs, is looked after by an old fiancée. 'You seem to have no other woman friend who cares whether you are dead or alive,' she says, and the words suddenly made not being married not sound like such a good idea after all.

But I can't lie around in bed moping all the time. My brother, for one thing, needs me. He's the captain of the MCC backgammon team and even though he regularly thrashes me at the game – I believe I still owe him a small sum of money – he nevertheless considers me a good enough player to be worth selecting for the league match against the RAC. I call him up a couple of hours before the kick-off and ask him if there are any keen substitutes who aren't feeling unwell, but he says no. As the elder brother I am legally allowed to tell him to go boil his head anyway but I don't want to let him down, so turn up to Lord's in a light fug of paracetamol and codeine.

The evening does not go very well for us, as it turns out. I lose against a nice Austrian who is, like me, a fan of Stefan Zweig, and against the opposing captain, who seems genuinely baffled at what I do for a living. This conversation occurs after the game so it's not as if he's trying to psych me out or anything. When I tell him I'm a book reviewer, the insolent pup asks me what it is about my opinion that makes it more valid than anyone else's. A few answers spring to mind, ranging from 'the money I get for it' to a non-verbal response involving the forcible insertion of a backgammon piece up his nose, but tonight I am an ambassador for MCC and must act the gentleman. Also, I don't have the energy for either sarcasm or mild violence. But it is not the kind of question, I feel, that it is proper to ask in polite society. Besides, I'm not well enough to answer it. And until I again find a woman who cares whether I am dead or alive, close family excepted, I wonder when I will ever be.

*

It is a chilly evening, the first really cold one of the winter, but the sixth frame of the snooker final between Higgins and Ding seems to have been taking all year. (There is nothing else on the telly except *The X Factor* and its spin-offs, whose mystifying popularity is one of the outrages of the twenty-first century.) Razors and I appreciate the subtlety of the Safety Game but this is taking the mickey out of the audience. The Hovel might be cosy and warm but the sense of stasis engendered by the snooker drives us to exasperation. We wrap up warm and head for the Duke.

The Guvnor, no doubt buoyed up by an Arsenal victory earlier in the evening, is pleased to see us. We have not been to the Duke for a while, because (a) it's been raining too hard and (b) we have no money. Christmas is bleeding us dry already, although how Razors can claim to have no money when he produces a bankroll the size of a baby's head is a source of some bewilderment.

We have also been (c) in somewhat melancholy mood. Love has been mucking us about recently, and this can get quite dispiriting. Let us propose, I say, a comparison between love and the pharmacopoeia. Imagine if some cunning scientist managed to concoct a drug which mimicked exactly the effects of love. The hapless user would experience, at first, a huge, giddying rush, besides which the highs of cocaine or crystal meth would be nugatory or even risible. There would be a sense of omnipotence and hyperinflated self-esteem which would at the very least render one a menace on public transport, let alone behind the wheel of a car. Against all compelling evidence to the contrary, the world would suddenly start to look like a place of boundless delight and possibility. You would, in short, go kind of nuts.

This problem with this phase is that it is of entirely unpredictable durability. At least with conventionally illegal stimulants you tend to know how long you've got before it all comes crashing down, and you can plan it so the next day is a day off you can use to recharge the batteries. With love you never know whether it's going to last days, weeks, months, or even longer. The hope, and indeed the idea, is that it should last until you and the beloved turn up your toes and die of old age, but, sadly, this is largely a fiction imposed upon a biddable public by a combination of vested interests (such as the advertising industry, which goes into overdrive to push the notion of happy families around this time of year) and our own wishful gullibility. In reality you can end up having your heart broken in a matter of hours if you play your cards right. And then heaven help you.

For if the highs of love can make you feel a euphoria comparable only to that of Soma in the Rig Veda, which was said to make you feel like a god riding the thundercloud, then the lows are correspondingly abysmal. Let us not dwell on them too much. If you are human you are probably familiar with them. You enter a kind of depression in which every aspect of life, and your own within it, becomes unendurably repellent. You neglect your personal hygiene. You forget to eat. You no longer do your exercises and you are too exhausted to offer your seat to ladies on the tube. It is like suffering, with no respite, a kind of existential toothache for which there is no analgesic except oblivion. You try and sleep for twenty-three hours a day – even though, the subconscious mind being what it is, dreamland is by no means an automatically pain-free sanctuary – and spend the intervening hour drinking more than is good for you. You also become something of a bore on the subject, and, on the whole, Good for Nothing.

In short, I add, warming to my theme, anyone who pushed a drug with these kinds of side effects would become a pariah even with the drug community. The forces of law and order would hunt the dealers and the manufacturers down with a zeal unmatched since the crusades, and even I, with my libertarian approach to matters of intoxication, would give them all the help at my disposal. Outside the courts, I would be leading the lynch mob, waving my home-made noose and shouty placard until my arms ached.

Razors and I become quite eloquent in our denunciation. Stefan the barman, who has returned to the pub as the fool to his folly, has had his share of knocks in this department, despite looking like a Greek god, and sympathises. The Guvnor, although seemingly immune to this kind of thing, is moved enough to let us buy large Lagavulins at cost price (a significant saving, for which we are tearfully grateful). Eventually, though, I slope off home. *Basta così*.

And then I get a rather interesting phone call.

4

New Year both is, and is not, a difficult time of year for those of us of an unusually feckless disposition. Although there is the nagging issue of resolutions, not one of which I have ever successfully kept, with the exception of 2007's resolution to smoke more, there is also the consolation that because they are largely meaningless gestures, it does not necessarily matter that they are not kept. This time, though, like molesworth, I have resolved to be GOOD and so I am going to damn well keep them, and if I don't, you can shoot me. This New Year's Day was particularly auspicious, for reasons which are not fully your beeswax (although it doesn't take a rocket scientist to work out that previous snafus in the romance department have resolved themselves in a favourable manner. Suffice it to say that happiness has returned, the wheel of Fortune back on its giddy cycle and for the time being, the right way up as far as I'm concerned), so I feel that if Providence is going to be kind to me it is only simple good manners to try and continue to appease her. (Although the Epicureans, of whom I count myself one, rejected the idea of Providence, I know the difference between a run of good and bad luck when I see it and I'm not going to risk matters by saying there is no such thing.)

First, the hardest one of all. This is the resolution that This Year I Am Going to Finish Writing My Book*, which has been an annual, and increasingly aggravating, institution since 1997. This hasn't entirely been down to my own indolence; it is also due to the fact that the subject, for which I received a substantial but long-since-spent advance, turned out to be of rather more breathtaking complexity than either I or my publisher had bargained for. We have since come to the agreement that maybe it would be better to write a book about something which does not involve my having to grasp every single aspect of popular culture since the dawn of time. So this year my resolution does not involve an excursion into the land of fantasy, and should not provoke those infuriating questions from my friends about How The Book Is Coming Along. Had I known how many times I would be asked, and how horrible it would get to be asked this, I wouldn't have started in the first place.

The second one is to try and be tidier. Actually, I already am tidier than I used to be but this is really to say not much more than that the site of Chernobyl is less radioactive than it used to be. It is, of course, still pretty radioactive. I am not sure how I managed to get this way, but somehow I can fuck up a room merely by sticking my head in the doorway. (If I want to render it uninhabitable, all I have to do is walk

* Ha, ha, as you might have guessed, as it turned out that year.

through it.) It is usually women who tell me that this is an unacceptable area of my character but when men start complaining about your mess then you realise it is time to do something about it. Razors (whose resolution this year, I gather from his Facebook page, is to start smoking) has been making the odd pointed comment lately, and when even I can notice that the dining table is covered in review copies and unopened tax demands then I concede that the time for action has come.

The third one . . . oh, hang it, I think those two are enough. I might, though, nod vaguely in the direction of restricting my intake of wine to one bottle a night and maybe even eating the odd portion of vegetables and . . . what's the other thing that the quacks say we should eat more of? Round things, like sweets but bigger and not as nice. Oh yes, fruit. I should eat more fruit. Razors sometimes buys these things which are orange and about half the size of a cricket ball. The name begins with a T, rhymes with margarine, and when he gets back from his hols I shall ask him how to peel them. I assume they need peeling. And I think the same applies to the curved fruit whose name begins with a B, I think. You know the ones. They start off yellow and then go black. Pineapples, that's the one.

*

Taking my free copy of the *Evening Standard* the other day, I see from the front page that Allegra Mostyn-Owen, Boris Johnson's first wife, is to marry a Muslim roughly half her age. Inside, she has two full pages in which to explain herself. I am, I have to say, delighted for her, and the whole business clarifies one of those strange episodes which can only happen to the divorced or separated man.

A few minutes after being given my marching orders by the wife, I turned, as men do these days, to the internet, in the hope of finding another mate. I started corresponding with one woman in particular, whose profile was not the boilerplate 'I love long walks in the countryside followed by curling up in front of the fire with a glass of wine' crap. After a while she confessed that she wasn't herself looking for a partner, but was actually a conceptual artist who was collecting men's own asinine and self-regarding descriptions in order to construct an audio-visual artwork. This, reader, added a new terror to the business of internet dating, but I did like the fact that she said my own profile and correspondence were not as stupid and creepy as every other man's. (She directed me to her website, which had actors reading out some choice entries, and you wouldn't believe how toe-curling they were. Apparently there are an awful lot of men out there who think it is acceptable to make themselves sound like borderline rapists with brains the size of bumblebees.)

Anyway, we continued to write to each other, and after a while, she kindly set me up on a date with one of her friends. Who was, it turned out, the aforementioned Allegra M.-O. This made me uncomfortable in about nine different ways, not all of them unpleasant (like all left-wing middle-class boys, I can find something exotic, even erotic, in the contemplation of the truly posh, and I can still vaguely remember the time when her face adorned the front cover of *Tatler*: look no further for an iconic image of all that was, um, debatable about the 1980s). For some years I had been proposing, in the pages of the *Independent on Sunday*, that her ex-husband was not who he claimed to be, but was in fact the construct of an exceptionally wily comedian, like Borat or Alan Partridge. (I once expanded on this riff at some length to Ian Hislop at a *Private Eye* lunch, and was most gratified to see the next issue using this as a basis for one of the magazine's jokes.) So, not only was I worried about whether I'd make some frightful howler with the cutlery when we went out for dinner, I was apprehensive as to whether she'd seen my little gag at some point, or whether I'd blurt it out anyway (I have form when it comes to making extremely stupid comments in a social setting, the all-time most blush-making being when I said to the late Ian Curtis's daughter 'You smile a lot more than your dad did'; you could actually hear the air whooshing out of the room as I said it).

In the end, dinner with A. M.-O. involved chopsticks, not knives and forks, so no class-distinction problems there, but the fact that she did not drink was a snag. As I have never been involved in a relationship whose successful prosecution has not at some point involved a decent amount of booze, this put me on the back foot somewhat, and the single bottle of beer I restricted myself to did not really help me overcome any social awkwardness I might have been feeling.

So the evening was a bit of a bust, but I have to say that I was quite impressed by A. M.-O.'s seriousness and sense of purpose (there was no trace of the eighties socialite on display that I could see), yet as I walked back to the tube, brooding on the strange ways of Fate, I suspected that wedding bells were probably not going to be on the cards. Now that I learn of her concept of the ideal man I feel a kind of relief, as well, naturally, as that sense of disinterested (I'm using the word properly) benevolence that comes when you hear that someone you don't know very well is getting married.

Some time later, I was introduced at a party to Boris Johnson, who for some reason had turned up in a twinset and pearls, with a wig the same colour as his own hair but much longer. I jumped; I think I may even have screamed a little bit. This turned out, on closer investigation, to be his sister Rachel, and long before I had had a chance to recover my poise and bearings – was this a new comic character, 'Boris"s Pauline Calf? – she said, in a way that I found deeply ominous, 'Ah! So *you're* Nicholas Lezard.' I wonder: why on earth did she say that?

*

Visitors to the Hovel are always amused – or appalled – by its eccentric features. Freed from the conventionalities, or the proprieties, of living in a home with a strong matriarchal organising presence, Razors and I put up with things which the married man would not be allowed to experience. What do we appreciate most? Is it the sloping floors, caused by the removal of a supporting beam some time in the 1960s, which makes the house as crazily tilted as a circus funhouse, so that every egg fried in the kitchen comes out in the shape of a croissant? Is it the bedroom window-frames stuffed with newspapers to keep out the winter draughts? The teetering piles of review copies, dating back to September 2007? Or the irreparably fused light fitting in the downstairs bathroom, which, along with its repulsive 1970s tiling scheme, invariably brings to mind the energy-saving slogan of those distant days, 'Brush your teeth in the dark'?

Well, visitors to the Hovel now have a new conversation piece, should they ever find themselves needing something to talk about: a very ugly fold-out sofa wedged immovably in the doorway of said downstairs bathroom. If you want to brush your teeth, or indeed do anything else except have a bath there (I was warned not to use this bath – not to be confused with the slightly less disastrous shower upstairs – on the grounds that, as I might have mentioned before, a leak has rendered the floor beneath it porous, and stepping into it will result in its falling into the kitchen below), you now have to climb over this cumbersome object.

As is so often the case, it is all the fault of good intentions. This is the sofa I've been sleeping on since moving in here. At first I was too depressed even to open it out. It's not a fold-out sofa bed; that would be too comfy. The back of an unusually uncomfortable sofa just folds down, leaving you with a crease running down its length. I have got used to this, as well as its hardness, having always assumed, for some reason, that this was good for your back (bitter experience has taught me that it is not). The cleaning lady has occasionally wondered why I don't swap it with the nice proper bed in the spare room next door, vacated, you will recall, ever since Razors smashed all Tim the Buddhist's crockery in a fit of rage, but that room is so tiny that it would be cruel to remove the only civilised amenity it possesses and replace it with this excuse for a piece of furniture.

Now, I can ignore a suggestion from the cleaning lady, much as I can ignore a request from the ex-wife, but I cannot ignore one from the Woman I Love, who has wearied of this sofa contraption and is, along with me, living proof that sleeping on unyielding surfaces is not, actually, any good for your back at all. 'You'll have moved the bed in here by the next time I come round, won't you?' she says. What with various childcare timetables between us, we can only see each other every other weekend, so I have been given, essentially, twelve days' notice to rectify the situation. So one evening, about an hour before she is due to arrive, I announce to Razors that we have become removal men.

Moving the bed out of the spare room is easy. I can even do it on my own. For the sofa, though, I need help. But as we move it out of my door and into the bathroom, so we can turn it slightly and move it into the spare room, it opens out again, as if possessed of a malevolent intelligence, and becomes stuck.

Razors and I have our talents, let there be no false modesty. He is very good at the cryptic crossword in the *Guardian*, and I can get the hard questions right in *University Challenge*, as I believe I have mentioned before. Three-dimensional geometry, on the other hand, is not really one of our talents; yet even we know enough to realise that we are, to use the correct mathematical terminology, fucked. We stand at either end of the sofa, taking in the gravity of the situation. The WIL is coming in half an hour, and all the books and other unmentionables – oh man, what a lot of unmentionables – that were living under the sofa are now strewn across my bedroom floor. Which do we resemble more closely? Laurel and Hardy, or the inept chimps in the PG Tips advert? I ask Razors if he minds if I cry for a bit.

In the end, I decide to cut my losses and stick to the part of the problem that does not require us to rearrange the very nature of reality. The sofa stays where it is, the room gets tidied up. Thanks to the power of love, a job which would normally take me half a day gets done in twenty-five minutes, the WIL is impressed that I even moved it in the first place ('you were either going to do it at the last minute, or not at all,' she says with just a hint of resignation; how well she knows me), and is even tolerantly amused at the Buñuelesque sofa, although I have a feeling it had better not still be there the next time she visits.

Later, my teenage daughter comes to stay for the week. 'Is it always like this?' she asks. Good question. 'Will it always be like this?' would have been good, too.

*

The important thing for that most absurd of creatures, the separated man in his forties, is to contrive as much luxury as possible for himself in order to mitigate the pain of his circumstances. I learned this in a hurry after queuing up a couple of times at the Tesco Express in Baker Street. It is a pitifully inadequate shop even if you are fond of Tesco, and I am not; its shelves are an antechamber of Hell, for nomads who have lost all hope. But there is, as Alan Coren once said, one good thing about Tesco: it keeps the riff-raff out of Waitrose. (He might have said Sainsbury's, but the principle still holds.) My Waitrose, in Marylebone High Street, is pricier and further away, but it does have a certain elegance. That is, as long as you avoid the section around the herbs and garlic. For some idiot in the marketing department decided that you couldn't buy basil leaves *tout court*: it has to be 'MAJESTIC Basil', as if no one would buy the stuff unless it was preceded by an effusive adjective. 'GLORIOUS Garlic', it says on the string bag enclosing two or three heads of what, if they were being truly honest, should be called 'MEDIOCRE garlic', or, if they weren't determined to infantilise their customers, 'garlic'. There are similar adjectives arbitrarily applied to tarragon, coriander, rosemary and the rest of them, but I will not list them. You get the idea. Oh all right, here's one: Rosemary is considered 'ROMANTIC'. Gah! (It is not. It is for remembrance, as Ophelia reminded us.)

In the days when I was both separated and without hope, I would have simply shaken my head in dull despair and moved on with shuffling gait, as if I were wearing down-at-heel slippers, to the dairy section. Nowadays, two and a half years on and full of beans, I find myself instead boiling with righteous anger. There is something soothing about it. 'So angry,' murmurs Razors as he glowers at some inane advert on the telly. (He used to work in the business and bad, stupid ads, which are the only kind that seem to be around these days, pain him dreadfully.) It is an infectious habit. Try it some time. It helps, of course, if you live in London, which offers the resident or visitor so many opportunities for outrage. Look at the tube map, which now, with a contempt for veracity which would make Orwell's Ministry of Truth whistle with admiration, insists that the Q of the Circle + Hammersmith and City Lines is still a circle. 'So angry.' (Lower the voice and the brow, as if you are a coiled spring about to release a terrible vengeance on the world.) Waiting in the freezing cold for half an hour for a 205 or 30 bus outside King's Cross because the 'Circle' line has been closed for the weekend? Repeat the mantra, softly: 'So angry.' Your fellow passengers (strictly speaking under the circumstances, they aren't passengers yet, they're those hoping to become passengers before they die of hypothermia) will treat you with respect and edge away from you in order to give you more room.

The poets understood rage, the need to vent the pent. How do those lines from Hill's 'Mystery of the Charity of Charles Péguy' go?

Rage and regret are tireless to explain
Stratagems of the outmanoeuvred man . . .

Or there's Donald Davie's lines comparing rancour to the indignant-sounding hoopoe. (I cannot look up the quotations and reproduce them with accuracy as the books they are from are in the increasingly entropic chaos of my study in the marital home. So angry.) Anger is aesthetic and therapeutic and, it is important to remember when writing for publications of the left, revolutions can't happen without it.

The trouble is, you find yourself wondering where to draw the line. What you might once have accepted with resignation or even complacency – such as an unusually cold winter, say – now becomes another stick of fuel beneath the simmering cauldron. It is the opposite of the hackneyed prayer to have the patience to accept what you cannot change.

I wonder if it is doing me harm, this new-found technique for resisting the idiocies of the age. Does not anger give you cancer, or something? *Au contraire*, I find (and, as Barbara Ehrenreich has noted, a positive attitude doesn't cure you of the disease, either). I feel and look younger than my years. If I was a dog my coat would be glossy, my tail would be wagging and my nose would be cold. But I really wish Waitrose would do something about the sodding packaging on their herbs. It makes me so angry.

*

Time, I am told, to clear out the books from my study in the family home. After about two and a half years it has been, I concede, long enough. Besides, not only is the ex-wife on my case, so is my daughter. A man can withstand one woman but two is too much. The idea is to convert the space into a bedroom, or maybe even two, for the boys. 'You, of all people,' says the ex, 'should understand the importance of a private space.' Whatever can she mean? I remember when we moved into the family home, some sixteen years ago, and I earmarked the loft space for my own workplace, Razors took one look and christened it 'the tug emporium'; it took me a while to work out what he was driving at. (When this column originally appeared in the *New Statesman* a rather witty sub gave it the headline 'Fiddler in the Roof', which I have to concede is quite amusing.)

But the place was used for work, too, and in it, on rudimentary bricks-and-planks shelving, I placed pretty much all the books I had used for my O-, A-level, and university studies. Here was all the poetry, all the Beckett, all the abstruse and recondite literary criticism. Along with God knows what else. I would occasionally wonder how many books there were; now, having shoved them into boxes and established an average number of books per box, I know it's somewhere between twelve hundred and fifteen hundred. This is not counting the books I am leaving behind, to be disposed of as my ex sees fit, or the ones which might prove useful or improving for my children, should they ever decide they want to dabble in literature.

So, tug emporium or not, it was, I always felt, the brain of the house. In our previous dwelling, I used to work in a room which had a view over the rooftops of northern Shepherd's Bush, and this I could find awfully distracting; I would watch our late lamented cat, Horace, beat the crap out of the neighbourhood toms and cheer him on. In the tug emporium I only had the bare bricks of the chimney flues, converging four feet from my nose, for diversion, unless I chose to relieve the tedium by staring at the bare white screen and its blinking cursor (or, before the technology advanced, the bare black screen and its blinking cursor).

As I pull the books from their shelves a familiar, ancient image comes to mind: and I identify it as Keir Dullea, in a spacesuit, his breathing magnified in concentrated panic, dismantling HAL's higher circuits in *2001: A Space Odyssey*. The process feels as slow and fraught. Will one of the three redundant, dusty computers cluttering the place up suddenly start singing 'Daisy, Daisy' and then spark into life with a message revealing the true import of my mission? Only now I already know the true mission: to move on, to move away, to let things go. I remember, as a child, seeing the film and being filled with what I was later able to identify as an existential horror, as I saw one astronaut's umbilical cable being severed, and he spinning off into deep space. It came to be one of the more relevant images I would use to describe, in art, my situation to myself. I think of my old companion: tropophobia; the fear of change, or, used specifically, the fear of moving house. Wonderful how the Greeks have a word for everything. It is somehow soothing to imagine Plato getting his chiton in a twist when he has to move from one of his caves just as he's become attached to it. Suffering mightily as I do from tropophobia this was a job I tried to put off as long as possible; that I can do it now suggests I have rediscovered a degree of psychic strength.

You need it, when you are taking deep core samples of your own past. Here is the letter from C — from 1983, which, twenty-seven years later, I can still not decipher as a love letter or not. Here is my copy of *Tercentenary Essays in Honour of Andrew Marvell*, the first book I ever bought in Heffers (£8.95? A hell of a lot of money in those days). What on earth was I thinking? I guess I read about three pages of it. It can go. Here is a box file of photocopies of my earliest published pieces, composed on a typewriter because they hadn't invented the computer yet. Here is my well-thumbed, and indeed well-frowned-over copy of Ezra Pound's *Cantos*. I would wave it in people's faces and say that all of literature was contained within it. Heavens, what a prick I was. In the box it goes; I'll come back to it one day.

I have been a nostalgist, though, from an early age. I think I was about eight when I first saw, in a redundant toy (an astronaut, as it happens), a charm and message which would only become louder through time. Early tragedy can do this to one. It is amazing I have managed to get rid of anything at all. But in the end we have to let everything go. There is no hurry, though. As I stack the boxes in my parents' loft, where the layers of thick black dust fall like the opposite of snow, I realise that, in the end, everything lets go of us. Whether we want it to or not.

*

I sometimes wonder whether public transport in this country is secretly run by the Lord's Day Observance Society. Or perhaps that weird Catholic sect, the one creepy Government ministers belong to, you know, the ones who wear rings on their thighs with spikes facing inward so they can mortify their flesh just by sitting down. Creeps. All of them. Try travelling from central London to Cambridge on a Sunday some time. No tubes to King's Cross from Baker Street. No direct trains from King's Cross. You can get them, I am told, from Tottenham Hale but Tottenham Hale is a frightening shithole even in high summer, let alone on a wet February evening. And one suspects the amenities on the platform would be less than satisfactory.

So first you get a train to Stevenage. Just say the word. Stevenage. You wouldn't be mistaking it for Casablanca, would you? You get on a coach parked in the leisure centre car park. A leisure centre in Stevenage. As Beckett once said about something else, not even Goya dreamed up such horrors. The coach is stuffy and overheated, a delightful combination, and the driver has thoughtfully decided to make the journey even more interesting by playing some local commercial station on the PA where the adverts encourage us to buy double glazing and the DJ plays songs from the 'irritating rubbish' section of the music library. The scenery outside, when you can see it, is ring roads, roundabouts, underpasses, pubs which may once have been nice but are no longer, and vast, empty roadside pubs which were horrible from the word go.

There is a high point at Letchworth, though, when we go round the first roundabout ever constructed in the country. No – in the world. I had been gazing at Letchworth, wondering if there was a more undistinguished town in the country, apart from Stevenage, and how long it would be before I killed myself if I lived there (I'd even spotted the flat I'd choose to do the deed in), when we approached the roundabout. Not very big – about twenty feet in diameter, at a guess – but, with signs advertising its historical significance at its noon and six o'clock poles, how large it looms in the psychogeography of the nation!

Truly, this is the omphalos, the still turning point of the twentieth century, which, I now know, began in 1909, when this marvel was first constructed. I once was sent on a bike ride from Los Angeles to Mexicali and back by the *Evening Standard*, in a group of thirty of us riding enormous Harley-Davidsons, and even though I picked up the nickname 'Crash' on the first day by coming off the bike on the freeway outside Chula Vista, which meant that, entirely understandably, no one wanted to ride immediately behind me ever again, I was accosted by a delegation of huge hairy bikers as we sat in a diner near the Mexican border. They were looking timid, nervous, deferential. Have you ever had a group of chunky experienced bikers, many of them wearing bandanas in an intimidating fashion, cough anxiously in postures of submission, asking for your advice? It is an ennobling experience. It turned out they had heard, or seen on the map, that there were to be roundabouts in Mexico, and they had never used one before. How, they asked me, were they to negotiate them? Just follow me, I said, and do what I do. They were more scared of the roundabouts than they were of me. I gather that roundabouts are becoming more common in the US but if you should ever want to terrify and disorient an American, just give him your car keys and point him in the direction of a roundabout.

Anyway, you then get on a train at Letchworth – we're still trying to get to Cambridge on a Sunday, remember? – and sit for ten minutes with your bladder bursting waiting for all the other lost souls trying to make this ill-advised journey. The Woman I Love – whose presence, I must say, has made this journey much more pleasant than it would otherwise have been – points out a sign which, if we interpret its simple graphics correctly, tells us that a saw, a crowbar, and a coil of rope are stored in a compartment next to the toilet. Under what circumstances, we muse, would you need a saw on a train? In case you felt like doing a spot of light carpentry? Or amputate a mangled limb? The crowbar's easy – that's for seizing and running amok up and down the carriage with, smashing windows, passengers' heads, you don't care any more, you're *so angry*. And the rope – that's easy, too. That's for hanging yourself after having spent three hours on a journey which normally takes not much more than one. Or if you live in Letchworth.

*

To Balham to see my friend Ella Montclare perform a set of unbelievably good trip-hop at the Bedford. Most of the people who have appeared in this work are sheltered behind decent anonymity, but Ella is a musician and could do with the publicity, even, she generously assures me, here. Which is not, as far as I know, going to be avidly read by A & R men anxious to pick up on the Next Big Thing, but you never know.

But I always find a stage magnifies people, and am awfully impressed by performers, particularly when in the proximity of people playing electric guitars, or when playing electric guitars themselves. Like many sad men of my vintage, I entertained, from the age of about thirteen on, not so much fantasies as certainties that I would be in a band. Indeed, I am still more than half convinced that had I gone to a proper comprehensive school and not actually been kicked to death for liking poetry I would have formed one of those well-regarded-yet-never-terribly-successful clever-clever indie bands, something along the lines of the Monochrome Set, say. (I met the drummer of the Monochrome Set a year or two ago and was *embarrassing* with awed respect.)

Sometimes, in an idle moment, I imagine my career trajectory in this alternative universe. The high point, I glumly realise, would have been an *NME* cover in about 1982. After the initial excitement our second album, *My Trousers Rolled* (or some other line from T. S. Eliot), would have sold two thousand copies, most of those after John Peel played the title track off it at the wrong speed. Then the 'musical differences' would have begun. By 1983 the bass player and I are no longer speaking to each other, and the lead guitarist, the one who can actually play his instrument, has gone off to form his own band, get Noticed By Brian Eno, and ended up becoming a household name. Things go a bit fallow until 2008 when, after

I have been making a precarious living in telemarketing for fifteen years, some bright spark uses our most famous track for a chocolate bar advert and we grudgingly reform for a comeback tour which attracts a small paragraph's worth of attention in *Time Out*. Someone puts some of the footage on YouTube and after two years this has attracted 632 views and one stalker.

Actually, all of these grand plans would have foundered on the impossibility of finding a decent drummer. Any fool can pick up a guitar, especially a bass guitar, but knowing how to hit all those drums in the right order and at the right time is something I find quite incomprehensible. The reputation drummers have for stupidity is, in my experience, undeserved. My friend John Moore – another person I name in full in the faint hope it might help his career – was for a while drummer for the Jesus and Mary Chain, and says he resigned from the band when the increasing vacancy of their lyrics got too much for him. He is still on good terms with them, though, and if you think I was embarrassing when I met the drummer of the Monochrome Set, you should have got a load of how I grovelled in front of the Reid brothers after meeting them backstage at the Royal Festival Hall. I blush to recall it – but then they are geniuses, not a compliment I use lightly. And I made a footnote in rock history by supplying one of them with grass at the aftershow party – even though it was in a non-smoking area! (I won't tell you which Reid brother it was but if you look at pictures of them you'll be able to work it out pretty quickly.)

But I suppose, all in all, I am happy with my lot. I may not have the guitar-shaped swimming pool in the back garden of my Los Angeles mansion – but I do have three excellent children, an uncorroded septum, half a share of a house in Shepherd's Bush, and . . . oh, now I come to think of it, I have a very splendid red semi-acoustic twelve-string Baldwin. It's looking hopefully at me right now from the corner of the Hovel's living room. I wonder . . . I wonder . . .

*

I ask Razors if he still calls it the Post Office Tower. He looks almost hurt. 'Of course I do.' *Après nous le déluge*, as I keep saying. I am *not* going to call it the BT Tower. We are the last generation who can remember the old money, what it was like when the Beatles were still functioning, when there was a genuinely left-wing party in power, and when that big phallic building was called the Post Office Tower and you could go up it – and even eat in its revolving restaurant.

I have a dim memory of having done so, with my grandmother I think; but I will have to wait for extreme old age, I fear, and the clarity of recall it is said to bring to childhood memories before I can remember the occasion in any detail.

But the POT loomed large – ho ho – in my childhood. Even now I find its sheer bulk at its base astonishing – how could something so pencil-thin in the distance look so imposing when close up? Yes, I know it is a matter of perspective, but for some reason not even the Empire State Building, on the occasions I've been next to it, makes me feel quite so insignificant, or the victim of some weird scalar inversion, like a character in a Will Self story. I had, for some time, a souvenir figure of the Tower, with a little plastic ring, representing the restaurant, you could turn round. For a while, I recall, I became radically unsatisfied with restaurants that did not turn round. The stationary restaurant seemed, to me, to be like black-and-white television: a maddening refusal to take advantage of the opportunities of technology.

But in the end that technology was turned to our exclusion. The restaurant closed down, ostensibly in response to the IRA menace (er – nine years after they exploded a bomb in the toilets), but, I suspect, because the spooks in the security services wanted to stuff it up to the eaves with surveillance equipment. (Its closure to the public in 1981 was an almost *boringly* obvious bit of mean-minded Thatcherism.) I once went out with a girl from whose bedroom you could plainly see the Tower; when I saw it from elsewhere I imagined it as a triangulation point, where our thoughts could meet if we both looked at it at the same time; frustratingly, the relationship ended before I could present her with this whimsical conceit (there's a Donne-ish poem in there waiting to be prised out, I think).

But now the POT is talking to me. Or rather, to anyone looking at it. '856 DAYS TO GO', it says. As I first noticed this when it was 926 days to go until whatever it is, this has been going on for some time. I imagine it refers to the reopening of the restaurant. Won't it be nice, don't you think, if when it finally throws its doors open once more, we are presented with the menu in the full splendour of its seventies heyday, prawn cocktail, Black Forest gateau, the works, and with diners being presented with frilly shirts and fat bow ties, should for some reason they fail to turn up looking like Jon Pertwee's Doctor or one of his assistants?

Of course, this is assuming that that is what the POT is telling me. It may well be 856 days to go to something else. All those microwave satellite dishes on the outside* invite the kind of speculations entertained by the clinically paranoid; and there is something unnervingly apocalyptic about the countdown. It may even be more unsettling than that. Perhaps the scientists have managed to tailor-make a message for

---

* Which have since been taken down; and now the building looks nude, emasculated, skeletal.

every single person who glances upwards. I am actually being told that I have 856 days to live; but the woman behind me is being told 'YOU LEFT YOUR CAR KEYS IN YOUR OTHER COAT' and the man behind her is being reminded that it is his wedding anniversary in a couple of days' time, and he had better buy a card.

Oh, damn and blast. A quick Wikipedia check tells me the countdown is to the Olympics. How incredibly tedious. Give us our restaurant back.

*

At King's Cross, starving but honour bound never to buy anything from Burger King ever again (a story too tiresome to go into in any detail; let's just say that I'm not so much angry with them as very, very disappointed), I go to the West Country Pasty Company stall and buy a sausage roll. My issue is not so much with the product itself, filled with some kind of vaguely sausagey molten goop which for the next three hours makes me think I have stomach cancer, but with the fact that as part of the transaction, the vendor – himself possessed of impeccable manners and winning cheeriness – keeps trying to hand me a receipt with my change. As English is not his first or possibly even second language it is hard to communicate my purpose to him as effectively as I would like, and a kind of stately but increasingly frantic hand dance ensues, as I try to extricate the 40p change from his hand without taking the accompanying receipt for £1.60, itself about the size of one of the old white £5 notes, only not as valuable or beautiful.

It is a very annoying phenomenon, this business of being handed a receipt for every single transaction, however footling and non-tax-deductible. One boggles at the kind of circumstance in which the retention of a receipt from W. H. Smith for a Double Decker or a Coke would come in in any way useful, unless it were to prove to someone that when it comes to outrageous mark-ups for consumer goods, W. H. Smith can teach the sommeliers of high-end restaurants a thing or two. But no. Instead one is handed this useless piece of paper along with one's change, for no discernible reason. I suppose the proof of purchase might come in handy if one were to be chased down the street by a store detective, but my shoplifting days ended in 1974 after a close shave with a handful of Fruit Salad Chews so my conscience about this kind of thing has been whistle-clean for nearly four decades.

After some reflection, I decide to blame Thatcher. Again. It is to her that we can attribute the rise of all the miserable specimens who equate life with sums of money. What arrogance it is, after all, to imagine that clogging up our wallets and pockets with these scraps is going to enhance our worlds. And how many of us, just so as to avoid making a fuss or looking like the kind of person who lets this kind of thing bother him, meekly accept this stuff and then let it fester, unwanted and forgotten, in our trouser pockets until it is too late, and we've done a laundry without removing them and all our clothes are covered in tiny bits of furry paper?

The funny thing is, I have recently become convinced of the good sense of keeping hold of the right kind of receipts. The reasons why I will keep under my hat until my accountant and indeed HMRC have said that I can break my silence without compromising myself, but the upshot is that I have now been spending my evenings sorting my accounts from April 2007 until the present.

This isn't actually my idea of a groovy night in but the surprising thing is that it is not quite so balls-aching as I thought it was going to be. Writers, on the whole, are antithetical to the idea of doing accounts, and consider themselves gay carefree spirits who flutter through life caring only for Art and Beauty. We are also not wild about our tax money ending up paying for an illegal war or rolled up in a banker's nostril, but do concede that some, for the time being at least, ends up with the NHS or whatever else this country does that it can still be proud of.

Anyway, here are my tips for the harried aesthete compelled, for whatever reason, to do his or her accounts. 1. Prepare a tracklist of good, fast rock music of an alternative bent (Wire, or The Duke Spirit). 2. Get drunk. As with washing up or childcare, accounts, done honestly, do not require a mind operating at top speed.

A pause, and a kind of footnote: I cannot begin to conceive what kind of lunatic optimism, or wilful, blind delusion, led me not only to write the above words but, for a period of some hours, believe in their message. This whole doing-my-accounts-schtick lasted for precisely one evening. After a very short while I got a bit bored, and to this day my accounts book is, apart from detailed pages for one or two months between 2007 and the present day, pristine, except for the handwritten names of the months and the years at the top of the page. Since then HMRC and I have come to a kind of arrangement: they get a debt collection agency to ring me up every month and ask for a largeish sum of money, and I give it to them, no questions asked. Everyone's happy.

*

It has come to this: buying a copy of *Men's Health* magazine in order to do something about my belly. It really is getting horrible; when I saw it in profile in the mirror, I actually screamed.

I remember how I used to mock the afflicted. At university, my friend Toby and I cried with laughter when we discovered an exercise wheel in our friend David's rooms – you know the kind: it looks like it might serve as a unicycle for a performing dog, but which you get down on your knees and push up and down in the most wonderfully undignified manner. Lord, how we mocked his bulk. 'You need a big hammer to bang in a big nail,' he said defensively. And now . . .

I am not quite sure how this has happened. I suppose if I raised my lifestyle up a notch you could describe it as sedentary, but in between periods of utter physical inactivity I walk miles a day and even do exercises. But for years I could get away with eating and drinking what I liked and enjoying Oblomovian periods of idleness. (Being too skinny, incidentally, was reason number 47 the wife kicked me out. Oh, the irony.)

So there I am, in the Co-Op with the Woman I Love, wondering if there's a copy of *Razzle* I can conceal this embarrassing magazine in. The WIL is broadly tolerant of my increased girth but she sure isn't going to stop me from doing anything about it. She goes in where I go out, if you see what I mean, and I feel it is only good manners to try and raise my game. 'Your Gut . . . Gone! Fat to Flat in 5 Easy Steps', promises the front cover of the magazine. As well as 'Sex So Good It's (Almost) Illegal!' There is a picture of a shirtless hunk on the front cover but his six-pack, as I believe they're called, is simply eurgh. What kind of crazy world have I stumbled into?

One in which what they say on the cover of the

magazine bears not even a faint resemblance to what they say inside it, that's what. When they say 'Fat to Flat in 5 Easy Steps' they refer you to an insanely complicated series of exercises spread over about twenty pages. The first thing you have to do, apparently, is find a Smith Machine and do something unspeakable with a barbell. Where, I ask myself, am I going to find a Smith Machine? Yes, I know, a gym, but I wouldn't go into a gym even if I could afford it, especially not looking like this.

I'm also not sure I have the mental equipment. I used to think that gym bunnies were on the whole the kind of people who cared more about their bodies than their brains but how the hell do they remember all these routines? I'd have to bring the magazine in with me and keep referring to it, like someone nervously following a recipe for the first time, which I don't think is the done thing. And when I am doing my dumb-bell seated shoulder presses I'd have to ask someone what the hell '8–10 reps' means. What is a rep when it's at home? Is it like a holiday rep, perhaps? I suppose this must be how people who haven't read a book since O-levels must feel like when they chance upon a copy of the *TLS*.

In despair, I turn to 'Sex So Good It's (Almost) Illegal!' This turns out to be 'Top stylist Bella Blissett reveals why your date put her outfit on, so you'll find it easier to get her to take it off.' There's something in another section of the magazine about orgies. The author of the piece, finding himself in that awkward position of being offered sex by a stranger he does not fancy, says, 'I spend ten minutes wondering if I could have sex with a forty-seven-year-old.' The fucking cheek. I am forty-six and ten months. I don't belong here. There's stuff in here telling men what to eat so they don't get strokes. You're meant to drink tea. This is good, I like tea. You're also meant, on another page, not to drink tea. A Friday afternoon quiz at work 'will increase your life expectancy by sixty per cent'. What, you mean I'll live to be 115? Michael from the Uxbridge Arms fell down the stairs after the pub quiz and nearly died there and then. Admittedly he'd had rather more than the half a can of beer a day you need to ward off osteoporosis. And unless I turned over two pages at once, I didn't see anything about how drinking a bottle of red wine a day will turn you into Superman. As Mick Jagger put it, and as I have had cause to quote before: what a drag it is getting old. But when you get magazines written by and for insolent brainless pups like this it's even more so.

*

A message from Razors. 'Don't bother coming back tonight,' he writes. 'The lights have gone out.' But I have to go back, as I have nowhere else to go once the Duke has shut. The Hovel, I have discovered, is unusually prone to power cuts, not, amazingly, because of its alarming wiring (although it is wonderful how much can be achieved with the judicious use of gaffer tape, which, as the botched DIYer in all of us knows, can also be used to mend cars). There seems to be something in the air, or more likely in the ground, which causes power cables in the area to blow up, and many is the time that a crew from EDF can be found at the street corner, drilling and running their generator well into the small hours. I have got to know individual electricians by sight, and the next time they turn up I shall bring them tea. They like it, I think, when I come down and ask them what's happened this time; once they've realised I'm not going to yell at them they are happy to go through the technicalities, and say what they think of their bosses. (Not a lot.) It isn't safe work: there are a lot of volts in those cables, and they have a decent fund of scary stories, and one half expects to hear a bang and find nothing left of one of the men except a pair of smoking, empty boots.

Razors, though, is no use at times like these. When the lights go out he goes to bed, losing all interest in the world like a parrot with a blanket over its cage. He likes to spend his evenings sending obscene messages across the globe and without a wireless router he loses one of his *raisons d'être*. I kill a couple of hours in the Duke and catch up on the latest gossip. It's all go there. Stay away from the place for a week or two and all hell breaks loose. The Guvnor's son, hitherto gay, now has an attractive Scandinavian girlfriend. (I thank my stars that I am no longer on the pull, for competition in this area is unwelcome.) Duffy, the manager with excellent taste in music, has gone, and been replaced by Darren, who is lovely but pronounces the names on the labels of foreign wines as if they were English words, and even then gets them slightly wrong, e.g. 'Coats doo roans'. His ex-girlfriend Ann, who let customers feel her breast implants and didn't know which band's members were Paul McCartney, John Lennon, George Harrison and Ringo Starr, but was still extremely popular, has left following a public indiscretion spectacular even by her standards and whose precise nature is best left unsaid, even here.

But in the end it's back to the Hovel, and darkness. Sweetly, if a little unwisely, Razors has left a candle burning for me in an empty wine bottle. You might find this hard to believe but we have rather a lot of empty wine bottles knocking around the place, and I also actually know where the candles are kept. I have enough juice in the laptop for a couple of hours but decide that firing it up would be against the spirit of the blackout, so I light a few more candles and settle down with a good book. (I recall the *Peanuts* cartoon where Linus reminds us that it is better to light a candle than curse the darkness, and his sister

Lucy shouting, 'YOU STUPID DARKNESS!' into the night. She reminds me of quite a few people.)

But I love the way a power cut can still be looked on affectionately. For people of a certain generation, power cuts bring back vivid memories of childhood, almost all of them benign (although I went violently anti-union for a while when one happened in the middle of *Doctor Who*). It is one of those times when one powerfully feels the absence of a piano in the Hovel. (This is another area where Razors could come into his own – during one of his many stints in prison, or perhaps in the army, he learned how to play. All I have in my repertoire, to my eternal shame, is an uncertain and room-clearing rendition of 'Let It Be'.) I also like being propelled back to an earlier time – a book read by candlelight seems better written, somehow, and if it's a book written before electric lights were invented, that's even better. I begin to think that power cuts should become a regular feature of modern life. And if EDF continue to maintain the infrastructure the way they do, they probably will.

*

Doctor Who with the children. This is an emotionally charged time for the divorced father. When people started tossing around phrases along the lines of 'Russell T. Davies has brought back family Saturday evening TV viewing' I wonder if they appreciated the depth or importance of what they were saying. Like Davies – he's almost exactly my age (albeit with rather more achievements to his name) – I grew up with *Doctor Who*, and can remember Patrick Troughton as the Time Lord (1966–9). I went a bit meh about the show after Tom Baker dropped out, although I respected Peter Davison's cricket jumper, but by that stage I had other things on my mind: trying to get laid suddenly jumped to number one in my hit parade of interests, for ever, and few girls, it dawned on me, were going to be impressed by boys who watched the show.

But when I had children, I became interested in what they might like, so when Davies brought the show back I was delighted that my then nine-year-old daughter, on seeing the first teasing posters with Christopher Ecclestone and the Tardis, said they thrilled her deeply without her exactly knowing why. It was then that I began to realise that what *Doctor Who* is about is not so much time and space travel, as alternative modes of fatherhood. Perhaps I had suspected this before. My own father, who on paper is the last person you'd expect to like this kind of thing, was as devoted to *Doctor Who* as me and my little brother (we also watched *Star Trek* together, and my mother, although American, would roll her eyes in exasperation when the cast staggered around the set in the pretence that the *Enterprise* was under grave, destabilising threat).

These roots go deep, as Davies must have intuited (his timing in resurrecting the show could have been tailor-made for me and my children), and it helps immeasurably that by pure coincidence, honest, when Ecclestone was the Doctor, I too had short hair and a leather jacket; after Tennant took over I was shoved into Converse – by the Lacanian, not herself a *Doctor Who* fan, as far as I ever got to know; and I flatter myself that my demeanour with the children has always been eccentric, otherworldly, and know-all, to the point that there was a time when the younger children could seriously entertain the idea that I could be, or play, a Time Lord myself. A notion from which I baulked at disillusioning them.

So we watched it religiously together, and I still recall the painful dissonance between the Doctor's supreme forgiveness of the Master at the end of the 2007 season with my wife's unforgiving rejection of me. Separation encouraging childish battles between parents to establish which is the coolest, I delighted to find myself, post-split, in situations where I could nab the autographs of Steven Moffat, John Simm (the Master), and Russell T. himself (not Tennant – the daughter got his after being taken to see his Hamlet), all addressed, by name, and with a little extra personalised note, to the children ('I AM your mummy!' wrote Moffat – a reference for Whovians there). In the case of Simm, I broke the Groucho's golden rule of not badgering celebs for their John Hancocks, but

I was drunk and desperate enough not to care, and he turned out to be an ABSOLUTE SWEETIE about it.

And now a new Doctor. I wonder whether he's too young for the part; that is, too young for my children to mistake him for me. They know I possess bow ties, but it has been an age since it has been witty to wear them. (I recall cycling down a street in Shepherd's Bush a few years ago in a suit, and some urchins – there is no other word – yelling at me: 'Fackin ell! It's Docteroo!' I've rarely felt so chuffed.)

Do not tell me I am the only man my age who has not thought about this, who has not felt this intimate link with the past and the future, appropriate enough given the show's promise of temporal possibility. Sometimes I wonder how different things would have been, how much less culturally connected I would be with my children, had this show not regenerated. I shouldn't have just thanked Davies for his autograph – I should have given him a big, fat kiss on the lips.

*

My mother's birthday. We have lunch upstairs at the Duke; very nice. The Guvnor may look like someone from Euston Films' darkest dreams, but he runs a tight ship and I can warmly recommend the asparagus with poached egg and hollandaise sauce. Conversation with my mother is like everyone's conversations with their mothers, but with a twist.

'How come you never tell me what you're up to, but you reveal your innermost thoughts and most shameful anecdotes to everyone who reads the *New Statesman*?'

'Well, if you match their rates we may be able to come to an arrangement,' I say. Actually, I don't say it. She has a point. My mother is a wonderful and remarkable person, but I suppose I do tend to play my cards close to my chest with her. She's usually able to guess what I'm up to, anyway.

On exiting the pub she expresses a desire to inspect the Hovel. This is something I have been putting off for two and a half years. It is not that it is disgusting – the cleaning lady, who is called Marta, but Razors and I now, in our heads, spell her name 'Martyr', has been in, and done her best, as always. ('Is this the worst place you have to do?' the Woman I Love asked her one morning. Apparently it was, if a rueful nod of the head and a wan quarter-smile mean 'Yes'.) It's just that I do not want her to see the evidence of my own failure so close at hand. Let me put it like this: the big news in home comforts this week is that I have found the eighteen-inch-long piece of wood that I use to prop my bedroom window open. Between this and the six-inch piece of wood I use to prop my bedroom window open, I can now prop my bedroom window open either two, six, or eighteen inches. Doubtless, using some combination of both pieces of wood, I could prop it open in even more variations of width, but let's not get carried away, three choices is plenty for me.

When my father was my age, he had two cars, a semi-detached house in East Finchley with a big garden, and a company directorship. (He had also, mystifyingly considering he once described Margaret Thatcher to me as 'a dangerous pinko', been awarded the Order of Lenin (Fifth Class), but that's another story for another day. He also studied Russian at Cambridge in the '50s. And yet he reads the *Telegraph*. How long is he going to maintain this charade of deep cover, I wonder?) Well, I have more hair than he did, but then I didn't have to deal with print unions every day, or have a son who at the age of eleven made a speech at his school's mock election urging everyone to vote for the Socialist Party of Great Britain. (Reflecting the SPoGB's level of support in the outside world, I got two votes, one of which was mine. I've always wondered whose the other one was.) But one thing about him you can be sure of: in his home, he did not need pieces of wood to prop the windows open.

Anyway, it is my mother's birthday, after all, and if she wants to see the Hovel she may as well see it now. It's not in a *disgraceful* state, after all; it is, in fact, in as good a nick as it's going to get, although we are going to get that fused bathroom light looked at one day soon, honest.

The thing is, I don't really mind living like this –

that is, in a place where people are always surprised to find that the kitchen sink actually has a mixer tap (some years into my tenancy here, even I am still surprised that the kitchen sink has a mixer tap. In fact, I even just went downstairs to check that this was indeed the case). In fact, in many ways, I have fallen right on my feet, or, like Brer Rabbit, into an especially nice briar patch. I wouldn't want the two cars or the big garden (although there is something cool about the Order of Lenin (Fifth Class)). I have never been acquisitive, and my circumstances now give me a chance to show just how non-acquisitive I am. But other people, particularly in the middle classes, do not think the way I do, and would see my circumstances as catastrophically ignominious.

There then follows a slow inspection. I forget to show her the terrace, which would have pleased her, because the view from it is very New Yorky, and, as I believe I have mentioned before, cinematically literate friends invariably remark that it makes them think of *Rear Window* – and my mother was living in the city around the time it was filmed there.

'Well, it's pretty much what I thought it was going to be like,' she says finally. Is that good?

*

It's that time of year when all sorts of significant birthdays gang up together: my mother's, my son's, the Woman I Love's, and, indeed, mine (all cards and cheques can be sent to me c/o The Guvnor, The Duke of Wellington, 94a Crawford Street, W1). The big sacrifice this year was to go paintballing with my eldest son and three of his friends.

Of all the things that make the man entering his late forties (forty-six can be counted as mid-forties; forty-seven can't) efficiently feel the full weight of *eheu fugaces*, paintballing must come fairly near the top. The last time I dodged behind trees firing pretend guns at pretend Nazis I was in short trousers, and even then our headmaster, Mr Cooper, himself a distinguished Second World War veteran, it was plausibly rumoured, told us off for making light of the pity and horror of war. We slunk away, chastened. (And then started again when he wasn't looking.)

Anyway, the kids are loving it. If you're a thirteen-year-old boy this is your idea of the most sizzling day out imaginable. And the paintballing company goes to some lengths to make us think we are experiencing something like armed combat. It is a strange mishmash of futurism and history: when in the playing zone we are obliged to wear goggles and helmets at all times, and we are in black overalls, so we all look a bit like scary riot police (it is disconcerting to see ten-year-olds dressed up like this), but in one of the scenarios we are invited to first storm, and then defend, a 'castle' called, in gothic script, 'Wolfenstein'; another one is called 'The Siege of Stalingrad' and includes trashed vintage army jeeps with hammer-and-sickle logos stencilled onto them. I crouch behind one and wonder what Baudrillard would make of this until a paintball hits me on the grille of the helmet and the paint splashes into my mouth.

It is, though, exhausting: running around the place and dodging paintballs in a black boiler suit in the April sunshine while carrying a heavy gun is not what an *homme de lettres* like myself is really built for, and after a while the sweat inside my helmet is running into my eyes, and, in the case of the left one, aggravating a rip in the contact lens to the point of agony. I give up. A very modern way to evade the draft, is it not?

And so to the optician. Here's another thing guaranteed to make you feel old. The WIL tells me that if you're over forty and either of your parents have glaucoma then the state suddenly rediscovers its nobler principles and forgoes its fee for an eye test. I qualify for this bounty. The eye test itself is much more high-tech than I recall. There's a machine that blows a harmless puff of air at your eyeball which still makes you flinch, and a peripheral vision tester which I think is as much a test of your concentration as your peripheral vision (I found my mind wandering, as it so often does these days, which must have affected the results).

A grim choice awaits me. Do I go for the stronger contact lenses which will allow me to, in the words of the Who song, see for miles and miles, but will render any printed text smaller than that in the *Mr Men* books illegible? Or the weaker lenses which might make me unable to read a bus number at fifty yards but will allow me, in bright sunshine, to read the *A–Z* unaided?

I go for the former option. Seeing for miles and miles is important: it buys one extra time to duck into doorways when one's creditors are coming down the street. However, this means reading glasses, which means that my desire not to wear glasses has put me in the paradoxical position where I have to wear glasses. (You can always tell those in denial about their ageing: they're the ones you see holding the menu at arm's length and muttering about the dim lighting in restaurants these days.) Consoling myself with the knowledge that Beckett, even after winning the Nobel, would get his from Monoprix rather than the optician, I bag a pair for £4.99 from the local chemist. If this isn't a milestone, I don't know what is. Anyway, it means that next time the balloon goes up and one is obliged to defend one's country while wearing black romper suits and armed only with paint-firing guns, I will get a cushy desk job. Or maybe, reflecting that I am now just one year off the age Clive Dunn was when he first played Corporal Jones in *Dad's Army*, volunteer for the Home Guard.

*

The Woman I Love decides we should hold a joint party. It has been some time since I have done this; I think I have to go back pre-children, which means 1995 or so. The family home was only just recently moved into and it was in a bit of a state, so it was felt that trashing it couldn't do much harm. It was quite an epic, round-the-clock bash, but when a woman asked, 'Please give me some coke, I have to do the school run in half an hour,' which is probably the single most disturbing thing I have ever heard said to my face, I decided that my party-giving days were over.

No such problems in this instance: the WIL is not only Very Firm about this kind of thing, but she wisely makes it a daytime (yet strictly child-free) affair at her house, which happens to be in Cambridge, so there is not much I can do in advance apart from come up with a design for the invite and let her know how many of my friends she can expect.

It is when she turns down the fifth redesign of the invite (I have got Razors to help, which isn't really a silly idea, as he has won shelf-fulls of awards from impressionable people in the ad industry) that I begin to suspect that there is a fundamentally different approach to hospitality depending on whether you are a man or a woman. I tend to take a laissez-faire approach which could be called lazy by some but is in essence pragmatic, partly due to financial circumstance and partly due to the fear that inviting more than ten people to the Hovel at once will cause them to collapse through the floors like the piano in the house full of jazz-playing cats in *The Aristocats*. So when I have a party these days I just tell everyone to come to the Duke at seven. (I got this idea off my friend Toby, who has been having his birthday drinks at the Uxbridge Arms every year since 1989. That he spends about 364 days a year there anyway does not, I think, detract from the blinding simplicity and beauty of the concept.)

But women are different. The party has to be a statement which says: 'I want to give you a good time in pleasant surroundings, and no, not the pub, my house, and I am going to work like a dog to make it nice, even if my nerves get shredded to bits in the run-up.' (Whereas the male approach to home-based hospitality goes: 'Well, the pub's shut; let's grab some glasses and go back to my place. Clean up after yourself if you throw up, and if you're going to have a fuck in the bathroom, don't forget to lock the door first.') The interesting thing is that I am now a changed enough man to see the point of this,* and quite understand when she hoovers the place from top to bottom, even the bits no one is going to see. Still, despite our having done all the cooking well in advance, she is in a pretty bad way about an hour

---

* I changed back later, as you will see.

before the kick-off, and requests a large, neat vodka, which she downs in one, something she has never, to my knowledge, done before, at that time of day. She needed something more than my continual reassurances that everything was going to be fine.

Well, you know what? Everything was fine. We were able to sit down and relax for half an hour before people arrived, and when they did, everything went like a well oiled machine. I know this memoir is meant to be a catalogue of misery and disgrace served up with a bitterly comic sauce for your amusement, but for once there is no misery or disgrace to report. The weather couldn't have been better if I'd personally arranged it with God to be like that; her friends got on with my friends, even Zoe, who has to take prescription sedatives whenever she leaves London, and her man the Doctor, whose strabismus becomes increasingly pronounced the more he drinks, and who has a fund of anecdotes which leaves unfamiliar and familiar audiences alike in some amazement that he is still both alive and at liberty. And you would have been treated to the sight of me picking cigarette butts off the lawn and going 'tsk'.

This is one of the most pleasant epiphenomena that I know: like streets that have had carnivals in them, houses that have parties in them are never the same again. There's always a lingering whiff of festivity that survives even one's drabbest moods. It's like they've lost their virginity, and grown up. As with the loss of virginity, there is a great deal of scope for disaster and humiliation. But when it goes right, it's magical.

*

I am in a very fancy restaurant, the kind which is obviously going for a Michelin star and has equally obviously been strongly influenced by Heston Blumenthal. My policy vis-à-vis very fancy restaurants is to shun them unless someone else is paying. And then, if in one, contemplate a corrupt and moribund civilisation. This is a special birthday dinner for the Woman I Love's best friend, though, and one look at the prices on the menu indicates that there is no way I can expect her husband to pay for us as well, however much I would dearly like him to. A second look at the menu indicates that I am going to have to live off baked potatoes and forgo the pub for the rest of the month if I am to recover from the gouging I am going to get at the end of the meal, and it is the beginning of the month. The staff are very nice but at these prices one expects not just good service but sexual favours from them. And not just any old sexual favours, either. Not so nice is the sommelier, who is ogling the WIL with such brazen intensity that I half expect him to tell her he has a lovely Semillon just from looking at her. (Obscene pun courtesy of *I'm Sorry, I Haven't a Clue*.)

But there is worse. I find myself in the unavoidable line of sight of a young couple opposite me. The woman is dressed in a burlesquey fashion and has permed peroxide hair, like a corny nod to Marilyn Monroe in *Bus Stop* but not as pretty. That's fine, though, I can live with that. It is her swain who is troubling me. It is not his relentlessly unsmiling manner – after all, as the first Mrs Lezard could indignantly attest, I can hardly wag the finger in this respect (strangely, but happily, restaurant silences are not a problem with the WIL, even though we have known each other since the first Thatcher administration). It is not the way he eats his food, which is mildly unpleasant, but not like Wodehouse's Roderick Spode, whose manner of eating asparagus altered Gussie Fink-Nottle's whole conception of man as nature's last word.

It is his hair, and his shoes.

The hair is one of those bewilderingly modish geometric cuts, a flattened diagonal ginger slab running from above the left temple to below the right ear. I do not endorse or even understand the vile persecution of those with carroty hair, and indeed such a hairdo would be an affront whatever colour its raw material, but this seems to represent an unusually badly thought-through approach to the vagaries of current fashion.

And so, as though compelled, my gaze travels down to his feet, and sure enough, on them are those equally bewilderingly modish shoes – the ones which look like something halfway between a tapered punt and a jester's shoe.

Now, as Mr Will Self once said, to suggest that any given style of dress is folly is surely the height of tendentiousness, given that few of us, were we honestly to examine our own history, can escape censure from the eternal style police, but he didn't see this plonker. As evil flourishes best when good people do nothing, I have half a mind to go over to him and beseech him to think of how he will wince at photographs of himself in this gear when he is older and wiser. But I don't.

There is, though, a certain fittingness to his presence in this restaurant (which will remain anonymous, except for me to say that it labours under a poncey pretend Latin name), for both plonker and restaurant exhibit a dedication to style over substance so decadent that it makes me wonder whether we are not, in fact, living very close to the End of Days. After all, you can't be ashamed, in years to come, of how silly you once looked if you are operating under the intuition that there will be no years to come.

As if to give solid form to my apocalyptic thoughts, a waiter arrives with a Kilner jar containing a small piece of fish and a cloud of wood smoke, which wafts away when he pops the lid open. Oh, for *fuck's* sake, I very nearly say. But at least I know I will savour my baked potatoes this month.

*

All I can think about is Liz Jones, the *Daily Mail* columnist who feeds her seventeen cats on cod (and, according to one report, organic Marks and Spencer prawns, but that can't be true). After confessing to being massively in debt, as a result of her mind-boggling profligacy (first-class plane travel, drinking only mineral water, high-end fashion, etc., etc.), and despite apparently being paid a six-figure sum not beginning in 1 for her column, 4,100 *Daily Mail* readers wrote to her, offering her money. Ms Jones clearly has enough psychological problems for a whole conference so I will not say anything nasty about her, but I must admit I am quite impressed. I've been making hints to my readers in the *New Statesman* for some time now and all I've received is a truckle of cheese, a £20 note, and a strangely fetching red shirt from a French charity shop. I suppose the *NS*'s readers are made of sterner stuff than *Mail* readers. And I had been told by the *Mail* that left-wingers were meant to be bleeding-heart liberals who believed in the something-for-nothing culture.

At least I am not as deeply in the shit as Ms Jones. I am also somewhat proof against the depredations of bailiffs. The only material possessions I own that are worth anything, I once wrote in my column, are a beautiful red Baldwin guitar and a laptop; and now I no longer, *pro tem.*, even have a laptop. Not that it would have earned me much on the open market. There is a weird permanent smear across the lower right corner of the screen, which is what happens, I have discovered, when you spill half a glass of port on the keyboard. The Q and A keys disappeared when a hardback copy of Albert Goldman's disgusting book about John Lennon fell on them from an overhanging bookshelf; when this happened I worried that every column and article I would be writing thereafter would be like an Oulipo exercise (think of Georges Perec's novel *La Disparition*, written entirely without the letter 'e'), but as it turns out, if you stab at the little plastic nub underneath the key you can eventually produce the desired letter. The rest of the keyboard itself is a mass of fag ash, tobacco strands, and miscellaneous scurf, and for some reason it connects to the web about as fast as computers connected to the web in 1997. And because I learned my craft on an old-fashioned manual typewriter, the space bar, which I hit unusually hard, only works one time in four. Now, after three years of horrific abuse at my hands, it has undergone a nervous breakdown and is currently being fixed by my great friend Toby, computer guru to the stars. (Although I did expect rather better. My previous laptop survived for ten years, even though it had viruses the way a ripe old cheese has mites, and had to be started with something not unlike a voodoo ritual every morning. And a matchstick.)

However, I would like to stress that from now on I am going to abandon all attempts to wring sympathy or cash out of my readership. For one thing, there are a lot of people much worse off than myself, and for another, Liz Jones has raised the bar for this kind of thing so high that there is simply no point in even trying to compete with her. I mentioned her case to Charles Boyle, who, as a poet and an independent publisher, knows a thing or two about being broke, and he said the real money is in donkey sanctuaries, because apparently the country is stuffed to the gills with rich people who are more moved by the plight of the decrepit *Equus africanus asinus* than of the, oh, shall we say, impecunious freelance hack. I toy with the idea of actually changing my name to 'The Donkey Sanctuary' and asking the layout people at the *New Statesman* to replace my byline photo with that of a particularly ill-used quadruped.* (I actually have form in this respect because I once went a bit mad when trying to finish a book in the countryside and started writing and signing all my emails in the persona of one Carrots the Donkey. I rather miss him.) But I decide against it. Send your money to Ms Jones. Her need is greater than mine.

*

---

* When this originally appeared as a column, they wittily replaced my byline photo with that of a donkey. Wearing Converse trainers, which were my mutton-dressed-as-lamb shoes of choice when my byline photo was taken. Lord, how we laughed.

I come back to the Hovel after a frugal evening out to find Razors watching *Junior Apprentice* on the telly. Well, he works punishing hours – nine till five or so, imagine – and so he's entitled to watch any old garbage he wants. Assuming this is chewing gum for the eyes and nothing he's paying much attention to, I take a phone call without leaving the room. So imagine my astonishment when he says 'Shh!' at me. Actually, I'm not astonished at first, I just assume he's joking. So after giving him a puzzled look, I carry on, and blow me down with a feather if he doesn't say 'Shh!' again, only more urgently. Blimey, he means it.

I conclude my phone call outside and then come back in and try to see where the appeal resides. What I see is 'Sir' Alan Sugar giving a bollocking to a dwarfish adolescent with, as Evelyn Waugh once put it, a face of ageless evil. Next to him is a larger boy who has unwisely decided to cover the entire lower portion of his face with bumfluff. On the other side is a young, fairly pretty blonde girl. I begin to understand part of this programme's appeal to Razors ('They should call this *Barely Legal Apprentice*,' he says at one point, a remark I pass on to you without comment), but surely that's not enough? I cannot understand a single thing anyone is saying, as they are all either talking in business jargon or mouthing vapid garbage like 'bringing something to the party' despite there clearly being no party in sight. But I certainly grasp the full, pure horror of what is going on: the unpunished corruption of young minds.

At which point we enter murky philosophical or even theological waters. Are these tiny capitalists being turned towards evil by 'Sir' Alan Sugar or were they already evil to begin with? Augustine tells us that evil is against nature, and that when God created the Devil he was aware both of his future wickedness and of the good that would eventually come of it. But I don't see any good coming out of 'Sir' Alan Sugar or his ghastly protégés. The dwarf I saw 'Sir' Alan shouting at was fired by him for no good reason that I could gather – he had behaved with the venal amorality which I would have thought was the indispensable characteristic of the successful businessman. And indeed, when being chauffeured away in the inevitable Roller, he gave us a tearful speech about how he was now all fired up to take over the world, and mark my words, we were all going to be groaning beneath his heel in twenty years, tops.

The thing is, you either have the entrepreneurial gene, or you don't. Razors and I once thought it would be a laugh to go on *The Apprentice* and give 'Sir' Alan a brain haemorrhage by both fucking up whatever stupid task he gave us and refusing to be cowed by his bullying manner (or else succeeding in our set tasks through intelligence and nonchalant charm, instead of acting like jerks), but we couldn't even be bothered to apply. Which perhaps suggests that anyone seeking to invest in our entrepreneurial skills is going to emerge considerably out of pocket from the association. It isn't hereditary; my great friend Toby, whose affability and generosity is boundless, is the son of a man who tried his hand at everything, from running hotels in Epping to nightclubs in Soho to a Diddy Donuts stall in, I think, Worthing. Not even complete lack of knowledge could stop him: he even, and I swear this is true, claimed at one point to have cracked cold fusion, and Toby once confessed that he had a nightmarish vision of waking up one morning, buying the papers, and seeing a picture of his dad accepting the Nobel Prize for Physics. I forget whether this was before or after the Diddy Donuts stall.

But it is going too far, I think, when people barely old enough to shave are being encouraged to demean themselves in the pursuit of a really superfluous amount of money. The question is not, as G. K. Chesterton said somewhere, of being clever enough to get it, but of being stupid enough to want it, and the desire to accrue wealth beyond an elegant sufficiency is the cause of almost all the woes of the world. Or at least the root of all evil. Well, that's one of the ways I console myself.

5

A rather excited message on the voicemail from John Moore, ex-Jesus and Mary Chain and Black Box Recorder, who tells me to call him urgently. He has decided he wants to start a cricket team and wants me to captain it. Although undoubtedly an honour, it is also a telling measure of his desperation. He wants to call it 'The Black Box Recorder Cricket XI', and seems unfazed when I remind him that Black Box Recorder only had three members (four if you count the drummer, but he never hung around after their gigs), and one of them, now his ex-wife, is a woman. Incredible singing voice, but not much use in the field, and I think there is some controversy about her bowling action.

'She can make the teas,' says John. 'She makes a lovely tea.' My suspicion that John is going through one of his manic phases grows when he says, 'We'll make more money out of this than we ever did out of rock and roll,' but then I recall how much money he's made out of rock and roll, and concede he might have a point. The thing about John is that, as a musician and songwriter, he is supremely talented, which means he is more or less disqualified from success. And this is a man who has performed on *Top of the Pops*. It makes me weep at the injustice of it all. I can never really understand why musically gifted people aren't always enormously rich, just as a measure of society's gratitude. I gave a quid to a dosser playing 'Edelweiss' on the harmonica the other day, thinking to myself, 'If you can play "Edelweiss" on the harmonica, how in heaven's name have you got yourself into this state?'

Anyway, I am always delighted to help John out. I sometimes wonder how he manages to survive; if ever there was a man for whom the term 'no visible means of support' was supremely applicable, it is John, unless he has a sideline he has not been telling me about, or has started importing absinthe again, which was never quite the big earner he hoped it would be. (I think he once persuaded the *Idler* to pay its contributors in absinthe for a while, and I remember earning a couple of bottles off them. That made for an interesting weekend.)

But I don't think a cricket team is going to be the answer to his problems, except in the area of *bien-être*. I play, not nearly as often as I would like, for Marcus Berkmann's team of heroic amateurs, the Rain Men, and each time I do so I love it more and more.

The trick is to negotiate that fine line between tolerating the inexpert player and wanting to win just enough to make it worthwhile playing in the first place. It helps that the Rain Men are all gentlemen, in the finest sense of the word. A few years ago I played for Harold Pinter's team, the Gaieties, and let me put it like this: the most welcoming and friendly of the bunch was Harold Pinter himself. The others looked at my ancient cricket boots, which were at the bleeding edge of sportswear technology in 1976, with astonishment at first, then derision; the Rain Men looked at them with something approaching envy. No, what am I saying? Actual envy. They represented, essentially, their whole ethos as a team.

A couple of Sundays ago, on the hottest day of the year, I stood for three hours in blazing sunshine as Hampstead CC's second or third XI hammered us into oblivion in a bumpy Hampstead Garden Suburb park. They provided a League umpire, which was quite impressive until he attacked the Foster's at teatime, and then, when we were batting, made some decisions which ... well, never mind. I made a plucky 6, taken in increasingly wheezy singles, which might look like a pathetic score but was in fact the team's second highest. The margin of defeat was so great that it went beyond humiliation. At the end of the day Marcus came round for contributions – £7 from each player. I thought about this for a moment, wondering if there had been some mistake. I had spent almost six hours slow-roasting myself in the sun, to the point where my skin had turned to crackling, my team had been massacred, I had been clean bowled by a bowler I thought I had got the measure of – and I hadn't had such a pleasant day since ... well, since the last time I played. (This is discounting, of course, days with the Woman I Love. Sometimes, of course, one can combine the two.) £7 to experience nirvana? Seems like a good deal to me.

But whether the Black Box Recorder XI is a starter, I'm not sure.* For a start, we are eight players short. John wonders whether he can get Wilko Johnson, which would be amazing, but he's in his sixties and if he's fitter than me that'll be embarrassing.** Any volunteers out there?

*

Plop! On the doormat lands a stiffie, inviting me to the party for the Orange Prize for Fiction. Further research teaches me that this is awarded only to women novelists. 'What?' I ask myself, quoting Borat: 'a woman has written a book?'

Actually, I know full well what the Orange Prize is all about, and indeed what the party is like. And not only that, I haven't quite told the whole story about how the invite arrived: a week or so before the event, I still hadn't received it. This put me into a bit of a paranoid flap. All freelancers know how easy it is to

---

* Would it astonish the reader if he or she were told that nothing came of this hare-brained scheme? I thought not.
** As this book went to press, Johnson announced he had terminal cancer. I salute him: a polymath and man of letters as well as an extraordinary guitarist.

be dumped, and although dropping off a guest list does not have the same devastating financial consequences as losing a gig, it does little for one's morale and can be seen as a harbinger of destitution. So I email my agent and Daisy Goodwin and anyone else I can think of with some pull to see about rectifying this distressing state of affairs. For, having gone to them for the last few years, I can confidently state that the Orange Prize bashes are the best of the lot. These days literary party invites are so rare that you have to go to each one just in case it's the last one that will ever be held. (Come to think of it, where's my invite for the HarperCollins summer party been for the last few years? Buck your ideas up, HarperCollins.)

But these are becoming more and more financially constrained, and even the thirsty critic on a tight budget can only sling down so much undrinkable filth before crying 'Enough!' and crawling back to his hovel, trying to get the taste of Chateau Batpiss out of his mouth. (Who chooses the wine, for instance, at the Hungarian Cultural Institute? We need to talk.)

But the Orange Prize, being sponsored by a phone company, is not going to be short of cash, and so they hold it in the massive ballroom of the South Bank Centre, which is not only pleasant in itself, but also has a large balcony where you can smoke until one of the security people comes up to you and tells you to put it out. Then, when he goes away, you can light it up again.

Then there's the fact that, for the first couple of hours or so, until I drink it all, they serve champagne. For many people there this might be no big deal, but it is for me. Not only could I only afford champagne if I gave up drinking, which would rather defeat the point, I do not move in circles where champagne is consumed as a matter of course. And neither, I suspect, would I want to. But this is not to gainsay the yumminess of the drink. And if Taittinger are going to pour the stuff down my throat for nothing who am I to complain? (I recommend the rosé, by the way. Are you reading this, Taittinger? Send me a case.)

But the best part is the company. Having long endured male-heavy environments it is an enormous relief, and a pleasure, to be outnumbered by women. In the days when I was on the pull or my marriage was disintegrating I found myself almost levitating with excitement as I passed through the throng of drunken, brainy women. Now I am not on the pull I can simply relax in the feminine atmosphere, and the general benevolence of the whole idea of the Orange Prize. I was worried when I first went that it would all be a bit Millie Tant and that I would be looked down on because I was part of the oppressive male hegemony. But it isn't like that at all: and the rhetoric from the podium always seems more sincere, more helpful than that at other literary dos which shall be nameless. Why do women do this kind of thing so well? Is it because, as Kingsley Amis once noted, they're really much nicer than men? It certainly feels like the benign opposite of something: the World Cup, I think. I contemplate the Gehenna of the footie pub packed full of steaming, puce-faced idiots screaming at a giant telly. Men.

I enjoy the Orange Prize party immensely, in the end, as I always do, even though at one point a nice young gel called Sophie sits me down near the Duchess of Cornwall so I can chat with her. I choose silence, and a discreet withdrawal. What on earth could I have to talk to her about? My thoughts about the redundancy of the monarchy? Whether I could cadge a cig off her? Her crazy husband? I think not. I don't want to end my days in the Tower.

I walk back by the Embankment in the warm night air. I've met lots of old friends, maybe even made a couple of new ones, but I can't, in the end, help thinking that there's only one woman whose company I'm really missing at the moment, and she's sixty-odd miles away, and asleep. Luckily, she doesn't give a monkey's about the football either.

*

An unwelcome call: Sebastian Horsley is dead. This is, to put it mildly, bad news. I got to know Sebastian after reading, and then reviewing, his memoir *Dandy in the Underworld*. At first I had considered him to be a bit of a desperate, attention-seeking prick (I mean, come on, a *top hat*); and there was something tragic about his botched crucifixion-as-artistic-statement in the Philippines.

But reading his memoir changed all that. He *was* a desperate, attention-seeking prick, but it was clear that he was very winningly aware of his own limitations, and in his ruthless flaying of himself he also laid bare the hypocrisies of others. When he heard that I was going to review his memoir for the *Guardian*, and favourably at that, word was sent to me that if I got the book review published there he would pay for me to have a session with his favourite prostitute. I demurred, not least on the grounds that accepting gifts, however unusual, and even getting to know authors, before the review is published is a big no-no as far as I am concerned. However, I was rather impressed: book reviewers tend not to get this kind of offer, or at least not since the eighteenth century they don't.

In the end, after failing to parlay the cost of the putative prostitute into a sum I could use to pay a friend's parking ticket, he bought me dinner, after meeting at the Colony, in a restaurant about six feet from its front door. He drank nothing alcoholic, and I drank plenty, but we got on splendidly. It is often, if not invariably, the case that the most scandalous art is produced by the gentlest people, and, indeed, Horsley's perpetually troubled look offered a clue as to his genuine sensitivity. People might have mistaken it for the perpetual offence the dandy takes at the vulgarity of the world, but it was clear that Horsley was ill at ease with himself, as I suspect many heroin addicts are. But he was, as far as my experience of him went, delightful company, witty in himself and the cause of wit in others, and I remember thinking at the time that this was definitely one of the better side effects of the collapse of my marriage (I have the feeling that the former Mrs Lezard would not have approved of Horsley, though she might eventually have taken to him).

We last corresponded less than a week before his death: he sent me a link to a *Spectator* blog written by one David Blackburn, who had written a pointlessly enraged and remarkably ad hominem attack on him. 'Do you know this cunt?' Sebastian asked me. No, I replied, and don't let it get you down; but the only indignity that Horsley saw in the business was that he was being reviled in the obscurity of a blog.

I doubt a nasty little piece like that would have been enough to tip Sebastian over the edge (if we are assuming that there was a certain amount of volition, conscious or not, in his overdose), but then perhaps he lacked the thick hide that is the indispensable accessory of the tireless self-promoter. I don't think he was entirely, or even at all happy about having a play made of his life; the top hat, which was, if you looked closely, made of cardboard, was a diversion, intended to fool your gaze into looking away from his own melancholy.

But he was sweet, as melancholics often are; and I think he would have preferred the term 'melancholic' to 'depressive'. He might have exasperated or repelled a lot of people but as he once told me, 'clearly marked personalities cannot be universally liked'.

It is a grim coincidence that he died on the day of Michael Wojas's funeral. Wojas ran Horsley's favourite drinking hole, the Colony Room. Much guff is written and said about the demise of Soho, and you can guess a person's age from the decade they say the Colony started going downhill, but as far as I was concerned the place was the bee's knees, and on a good night going there was like turning up to a really good party to which you had not been invited, but which was delighted to see you anyway. (You could even smoke in there, up until the time that the stupid lead singer of Razorlight blabbed excitedly about this in an *NME* interview; the next day the place was raided by the police.) That we have allowed the Colony Room to be swallowed up by property developers shows what mediocre caretakers we are of our own heritage. And as for Horsley letting his own life slip through his fingers like that – well, if it wasn't deliberate (and I don't think it was) then it was unforgivably stupid. Not that he would have been bothered by the judgement, were he in a position to hear it.

*

When spirits are down and the pubs are shut, nothing quite lifts the heart like a game of night cricket. This is decided by Razors at about two or three in the morning – due to the amount we've been drinking, I'm not really even sure what day of the week it is any more, let alone what time of day – and it seems like a splendid idea, and besides, it's been a long time since we've played it, and I want to see how the new Kookaburra ball I bought the other day performs when it's been scuffed up a bit.

There's a lovely square by the church in the street where I live and sometimes I play with the boys against its wall with a tennis ball. One bowls from the sign which advises against ball games, just to let my children know that rules are more like guidelines than hard and fast injunctions – although what the sign says, if you follow the small print, is that playing ball games there is only an offence if the game in question is bothering someone else. It is nice to know that nuance is still respected in some tucked-away corners of the by-laws. Besides, only the most joyless officious jerk would not warm to the sight of a man playing cricket with his young sons in the summer sunshine. Actually, once, someone did object. He was Austrian, it turned out, and was old enough to have been doing something questionable, albeit probably only in short trousers, at some point in the early-to-mid-1940s, and although I might have been unfairly insinuating something when I said 'Ah' meaningfully when he explained his provenance, no further complaint came from him. Sometimes passersby join us, once even a group of backpackers from some Eastern European country – Slovakia, perhaps – and I like to think that when they go back to their homeland they say something along the lines of 'What a wonderful, eccentric and idyllic game we played that afternoon with that silly little man and his delightful boys. Let's learn the rules properly and thrash the English at it in ten years' time.'

But real night cricket, I concede, is another matter. To be fully appreciated it is played with a proper hard, red ball, a real bat, and no sissy stuff like helmets, pads, boxes or gloves. Now you begin to see why it's only played well after licensing hours. (The ambiguity of that sentence is deliberate.) The stumps I chalked up in April are beginning to fade but if you stare at the wall long and hard enough you can see them faintly and take some sort of guard.

Not that there's much point in doing so. I have always found that after about midnight one's radar goes and the aim becomes as erratic as Steve Harmison's on one of his worse days. This is a good thing. Razors, whose bowling action was apparently learned from watching Jeff Thomson in 1975 and has only been modified by the addition of a suspect bend of the elbow which would make the finicky umpire no-ball him with every delivery, tends not to get the ball anywhere near the bat, which is just as well as it is awfully hard at the best of times to pick out the red ball against the sodium-lit night, and even harder after a bottle or two of Shiraz. In fact when he is bowling the safest place to stand is bang in front of the stumps. Eventually I weary of flailing at an invisible target and hand the bat to Razors so he can have a go. After all, hitting things is what he loves doing above almost everything else, and I like to see him happy.

Funnily enough, my bowling has sharpened up. I contracted a bad case of the yips a couple of years ago when it came to bowling, to the extent that I am reluctant to do it even in the nets, but sometimes a wee drinkie helps loosen up the muscles and build confidence. I clean bowl Razors a few times, I am convinced of it, but let him carry on until he gets his eye in and starts connecting, wellying the ball all over the place with a vengeance. It is at about this time that we notice the police helicopter hovering overhead.

I also notice that there are some tramps, or perhaps extremely tired and dishevelled Slovakian backpackers, asleep on the steps of the church, and even in my state I think that they might not appreciate being woken up or possibly killed by a rogue shot, so I halt proceedings while I suggest we look for another pitch. And besides, that helicopter is really beginning to get on our tits. (I'm not that worried about the Old Bill. The last time they stopped us from playing in the middle of the street at three in the morning, I waved my MCC hankie at them, and they just told Razors to get me home safely, as I seemed a little tired.)

In the end we find a charming mews which has a nice line in acoustics. As almost everyone except us who lives in Marylebone has far too much money for their own good I'm fairly insouciant about this. Besides, one can imagine someone waking up and thinking, 'As only a pair of certifiable maniacs would be playing cricket out there now, I must be dreaming.'

In the end, the ball rolls irretrievably between the steel bars of the underground car park. Razors gives the police helicopter one last V-sign, and I reflect that the two of us have a combined age of ninety-three.

*

The weather is being a bit silly right now, alternating between rain and brightness, but I still have fond memories of last week's mini-heatwave.

Londoners fall into two distinct camps here: those who revel in the heat, and those who loathe it. There would appear to be no middle ground. My poor friend the Moose cannot bear high temperatures, and calls the weather 'beastly'; those who come from honest British yeoman stock such as him tend to suffer, whereas I, with the blood of at least three southerly races and nations in my veins, delight in it. I remember how pleased I was to discover that the French verb *lézarder* means 'to bask'. Did my ancestors pick their surname on purpose, or was it bestowed upon them? It is worth, I have learned, a bit of unimaginative teasing at school to have a name that describes what you do, like being a Cooper and still making barrels. 'This is what lizards like doing in the heat, and so do we,' is the message my forefathers are sending down the generations, and who am I to argue with that?

I love it when it is too hot, when the decomposing rubbish starts to remind you of the smells of Moroccan souks, when the air becomes almost liquid, and you can cultivate a really striking watchstrap mark. I colour easily, and take a perverse pleasure in making people think I've been to Egypt when all I've done is loaf about in the sun, or, at my most strenuous, play cricket or go punting. The heat makes me do unusual things, like drink white wine or buy pots of basil.

And so it is with all this in mind that the Woman I Love and myself head off to the park. Although she looks rather more like she has Viking ancestry than I do, she, too, worships the sun. We had been planning on going to St James's Park, but it is too hot to go any further than about half a mile, so I take her to the Broadwalk, one of my favourite parts of Regent's Park, a colonnade of sculpted trees and spectacular flowerbeds which I hope she will be able to identify for me. Among her other talents, she is a gifted and knowledgeable gardener, with a talent for inspiring enthusiasm even in me. I have taken to watering the pots on the Hovel's terrace, although these at the moment contain nothing much more than used tealeaves, grass, thistles, some fairly pretty weeds, and in one a plant which recalls nothing so much as the tree, in the second act of *Godot*, with 'four or five' leaves on it. I like to think I am getting into good habits, and, besides, this is a kind of existential garden, or, if you prefer, a Darwinian garden, where only the plants most fitted for this harsh environment can survive (there's some lavender in one of the pots; how that got there I can't imagine).

After only half an hour even I find myself thinking about heatstroke, and thinking of moving on. We are lying by one of the fountains and I am reluctant to use the recycled pondwater, green even as it gushes from the pipes at the base, to wet my hair, but I do anyway. Doing so more than once might invite catching something from the ratty pigeon bathing himself in the fountain's highest bowl. We get up and walk along the avenue until we get closer to a crowd which from a distance we had thought was a queue for an ice-cream stand.

It turns out to be an audience surrounding a parquet floor. And then, after a brief announcement, the audience moves onto the floor and becomes a crowd of dancers. The music is a waltz, a tune of rudimentary schmaltz produced by a synthesizer – and yet it is bewitching. The couples dancing are stately, serious, rapt in their own technique and ability. They are young and old; gay and straight. One couple wear, below their casual shorts, patent leather dancing shoes. The floor is crowded but there are no collisions.

The spectacle is mesmerising, surreal, like something from a dream sequence, or a moment of pivotal elegy in a film; I wonder if I have already seen it and forgotten. The WIL nails it for me: there's a climactic scene set here in one of our favourite novels, Howard Jacobson's *The Act of Love*.

The effect is strange, as if the traffic between reality and its representation has become reversed: the heat, drowsiness, and meta-fictionality combine to make me feel thoroughly, but pleasantly spooked, as if we had become our own Alices, dozing on the bank.

However, I think as we walk slowly back to the Duke for a beer, the day I learn how to dance like that – that's when I'll know I've fallen down the rabbit hole.

*

To *Toy Story 3* with the children. I know enough by now about my own state of mind and the efficiency with which the good people of Pixar can churn the human heart, so I am bracing myself. In what proves to be only the first of many emotional moments during the course of the afternoon, I find that the cost of taking myself and three children to the cinema at Westfield is over £70. There is a cheaper cinema in the run-down shopping complex on the other side of the Green, but perhaps deliberately, it is not showing the film at the only time I can make it without removing the children from school. As I stumble, ashen-faced, from the counter, one of the children says, 'You've won!' meaning, it turns out on enquiry, that it is I, and not their mother, who have 'won' the honour of taking them to see this film, which they have been looking forward to for some time. Not having been aware that there was any contest in the first place, I murmur to myself the words of the Greek, 'another victory like that and we are done for.'

As for the film, I am well aware that age has softened both my head and my heart. I think it has something to do with having children. Once, when we were on a somewhat idealist mission to have the eldest child grow up bilingual, we got hold of a video of *101 Dalmatians* (the original Disney cartoon) in French. For some reason this gave the film an added poignancy, and whenever I watched it with the eldest I would find myself in bits by the time Pongo manages to get his owner married. Which is fairly early on.

This trend of getting emotional at the movies continued. Everyone cries at the beginning of *A Matter of Life and Death*, but I realised things were getting out of hand when I found tears trickling down my face at the end of *Wallace and Gromit: The Curse of the Were-Rabbit*. As for the *Simpsons Movie* – don't get me started. (The image of Homer Simpson adrift on an ice floe in the shape of a broken heart haunts me to this day, to the extent that I am not sure if I am the same man I was before I saw it.)

Anyway, to the entertainment. It turns out that the reason the tickets were so expensive is because the cinema is a luxury one: the screen is larger than the typical glorified TV screen of the modern multiplex, and the seats are larger than the average armchair, with softly glowing panels upon which you can rest your drink and your popcorn. (Which, wise now to the grasping ways of cinema operators, I have instructed the fruit of the Lezard loins to buy on the Uxbridge Road and then smuggle in themselves.) This is all quite exciting, and I have been intrigued by a review of the film by a critic I respect which said it was, all things considered, 'disappointing'. Disappointing, eh? Good – less chance for me to be turned into an emotional wreck by the end.

Ah. With all due respect to the critic concerned, he did not see this film with three children of his own, all of whom are bringing with them their own memories and expectations (they have, literally, grown up with the first two *TS* films; my eldest is as old as the first *Toy Story*). Just as the toys in the film are not just toys, but concentrations of childhood and nostalgia for it, so children are more than just your offspring, and their own beings: they are, inadvertently, what you invest them with as well.

I have to salute the ingenuity of the film's creators. Even allowing for the fact that I'm a sentimental old fool, they sure know how to put an audience through the wringer. At one point I realise that I am not so much watching a movie as submitting myself to a ruthlessly efficient machine for making people cry. I am not sure whether this is an advance or a regression in the art form. I try and look at the film as a Marxist critique on disposable capitalist society (although like all children's films, it's hard-core conservative); I dredge up some mangled Lacan with which to interpret its themes of loss and desire. I even try and distract myself by contemplating Barbie's disturbingly cute bottom.

But it is no good. The final minutes of the film (which comes after scenes of such infernal distress that I wonder whether young children should even be allowed to see it), as Andy hands over his toys to a younger child, and then, in a moment for which all the toys have been yearning for years, plays with them for one last time, have been almost sadistically crafted to prompt sobs. It is perhaps only this realisation that stops me from losing it altogether. As we leave, shattered, I resolve to watch something more soothing next time with them. Like *Psycho*.

*

The school holidays. Jesus wept. Because booking things months in advance is not exactly my strong suit, this involves schlepping back and forth between the Hovel and the family home in Shepherd's Bush. It's like the opposite of commuting, or a weird variant of it: travelling not from home to office and back, but from home to sort-of-home and back.

It is odd spending the week in the home in which my three children were born and raised. I know every inch of it: I sanded half the floorboards, painted half the window-frames, and there are still some sections of wall in which my initial colour scheme, bold, original, yet tasteful, has not been edited out of history. Three years on, there is still some of my crap waiting to be chucked out: eighteen boxes of books and stuff, some twenty to thirty per cent of the total, which I would like to keep but which I don't have space for. (The rest, as I mentioned earlier, is gathering dust in my parents' loft, and they say they would rather not have any more, as they don't want their house to collapse on top of them. Fair enough.) It sits, hulking sullenly in the living room, behind me as I type. It's strange leaving the place to go back to the Hovel every day: saying goodbye to the children is far less pleasant than I let on, even if I know I'm going to be seeing them the next day. The melancholy generally lasts, I have discovered, until I get halfway up the escalator at Marble Arch.

Still, it is a delight to see them. By not being exposed to a grumpy father 24/7, they seem to have turned into rather splendid young people, if I may say so myself. Who knows? Their mother may even have had something to do with it. And as I have never been the kind of father who says anything even remotely like 'Let's go camping,' they do not mind it if we basically slob around all day. But there is still the problem of how to keep them entertained, to get them off the PlayStation (have you seen *Call of Duty 6*? It's a bit disturbing, frankly). Open to suggestion, I am pleased to receive a text from their mother. 'Why don't you take them out on a pedalo on the Serpentine?' it says.

In theory, and with normal children, not to mention a normal father, or the kind of father you get in adverts, this is a perfectly good idea, and I think it is rather nice that she is giving me ideas about what to do with them, for, like many men, I have little imagination when it comes to entertaining children, and am seized with that brain-freezing mixture of panic and shame which is what we feel when our limitations are made manifest to us. To make matters worse, my children suffer from great inertia. Maybe they're like little balls of lightning when they're with their mother, but when they're with me you have to scrape them off the floor with a shovel. With negotiation, one can get them to play a bit of cricket in the scary park down the road, and I think I might persuade them to play some poker later on, but trying to get a fifteen-year-old girl and thirteen-year-old and ten-year-old boys to agree on a common agenda is a tall order indeed. There's also the problem of getting them to the Serpentine, getting them dressed so they can go on public transport to go to the Serpentine without causing a scandal, and indeed prising them off the sofa so they can get dressed . . .

Anyway, there is a new development afoot. The youngest boy has come down and asked his sister where the first *Harry Potter* book is. This is really quite astonishing, as he is not really the kind of boy who picks up books unless they are heavily illustrated with pictures of space. Nothing wrong with that, of course, space is cool, but by his age I was halfway through *Middlemarch* and could address the cats in Latin hexameters. (This is actually a monstrous fib. At his age I was playing Owzat and/or seeing how many times I could bounce a ping-pong ball on a bat before losing concentration, when I had the time to spare. 1,069 times, since you don't ask.) Now, I feel, is not the time for me to start on my critique of J. K. Rowling's prose style.

So when Eldest Daughter comes down and says that the Youngest Boy is actually reading, we are both conscious of the scale of the achievement, and, at the same time, its precarious nature. 'It's like when a butterfly lands on your arm,' she says. 'You have to be completely still or it's all over.'

It is a tricky business. There are builders noisily converting the attic. The boys' eleven-year-old cousin is staying over. There are electronic games and apps and whatnots in three or four different formats, offering the chance to do everything from kill the Taliban to play for Arsenal. We hold our breath. The butterfly is still there. But for how long?

*

I have become half-obsessed with Stephen Moffat's excellent updating of Sherlock Holmes for the BBC of late. At the time of writing I have seen only the first two episodes, back to back (three solid hours of red-hot non-stop sleuthing action!), but am very impressed. And to think I might have missed it, had not various people alerted me to the fact that Holmes and Watson's modern-day pad looks exactly like the Hovel. Well, it's not exactly like the Hovel really, but there are similarities. We do not have skulls everywhere but the Hovel is near Baker Street and the house is of the same vintage. We do not have a Mrs Hudson but we do have Marta the Martyr.* Razors and I do not solve crimes but we do do a certain amount of sleuthing. There was The Case of the Missing Corkscrew, The

---

* In the intervening months, Marta and I have exhausted the

Adventure of the Purloined Chinese Takeaway, and The Enigma of the Insane Women. (The answers to which were, respectively, under or behind the pile of newspapers and books on the table, en route on the back of a moped from the Sizzling China takeaway emporium, and, well, as for the last, that, like the case of the Giant Rat of Sumatra, that is a story for which the world is not yet prepared.) We also have a mirror above the fireplace stuck all over with Post-It notes, which admittedly are not significant clues but are instead plot ideas for the hugely amusing sitcom we are going to write about the Hovel.

At least, we used to have a mirror plastered with Post-It notes until one day Marta decided they were rubbish, literally or figuratively we do not know, and threw them all away. Well, they had been hanging

---

scant reserves of our conversation. It now consists of a hello, an offer of a cup of tea, usually but not invariably declined, a brief talk about the amount I owe her for various cleaning products, the handover of cash and an amicable farewell. I am quietly ashamed of this quintessentially English behaviour, and even more so when Amel, visiting from Paris, has a talk with her when I am on an errand, and discovers that, for some reason, Marta thinks surprisingly highly of me. Why this should be so is something of a mystery, unless she appreciates my silent reserve and the fact that I do not grope her or yell at her. To which one can only say that it is a sorry state of affairs when not-groping and not-yelling are seen as positive character traits in themselves, when I thought they were simply the bedrock requirement for inclusion into the human race.

around for a while, doing nothing much except multiplying, but there were some good ideas there. 'They decide to start an escort service' looked promising, as did 'they try to amuse themselves in a blackout', although the most conceptually ambitious one, 'they're dead', was stolen by the people who did *Ashes to Ashes*. But if one day we hear of a brilliant new Romanian comedy about the misadventures of a couple of divorced middle-aged bums we'll have a good idea who's responsible.

But there is an added poignancy to my appreciation of the new Sherlock Holmes. Like the original, it begins with Holmes's search for a new housemate. And, in news more distressing than either of us can bear, Razors, my compañero of two years and good friend for seventeen, is leaving. For New York, where he has been unaccountably offered a job. The selfish bastard wants to be on the same continent as his children, and earn twice as much money, and, who can blame him, put the Atlantic between us. It also turns out that he has been sitting on this bombshell for two weeks, unwilling to upset the fragile ornament that is my peace of mind.

It is the end of an era. Two years living in each other's pockets and never a cross word except in jest. We have hidden our vegetables under our cutlery together, bought each other Lagavulin for Christmas without prior arrangement, simply because we knew our own, and each other's, minds. I smile indulgently when he lobs empty bottles of wine under the chaise longue. No more the night cricket; no more the pints of chilled cider while we shoot the breeze outside the Duke. When he makes outrageously perverted comments about the woman who reads the weather on the local BBC news I do not report him to the authorities. He was (although he hotly insists the converse) the Falstaff to my Shakespeare, and, indeed, the Watson to my Holmes, the . . . well, fill in the names of any of the great British cultural and comic dyads. We have heard the chimes at midnight and plucked the gowans fine. Am I, it suddenly occurs to me in horror, the Withnail to his Marwood, to be left reciting *Hamlet* to the wolves in Regent's Park?

So, like Holmes, I am on the lookout for a new person to share the Hovel with. Finding a replacement for Razors is not going to be easy, for that person is going to have to have a very laissez-faire attitude to fixtures and fittings in the bathroom and kitchen, not be a dogmatic believer in floors and stairs that are one hundred per cent horizontal, and exhibit a tolerant attitude to mice. (We have not seen or heard Mousey for some time, but you never know when he'll be back.) More to the point, they are going to have to have a very tolerant attitude to me. I mischievously look forward to holding a set of interviews *à la Shallow Grave*, and if I end up with Keith Allen dead on his bed with a pile of money that'll be fine by me. (One day I will tell the world the story about

Keith Allen and the Zippo, a tale which, when it is finally revealed, will be as fatally damaging to his good name as that of Sir Gregory Parsloe-Parsloe and the prawns.) On the plus side, it's near Baker Street, and there is a Majestic Wine within staggering distance. Form an orderly queue.

6

I stumble downstairs on a muggy, sultry morning to find, miles from his natural habitat, an adult bull walrus asleep on my sofa. This is unusual, even for the Hovel, which, like the Hellmouth in *Buffy the Vampire Slayer*, is a vortex for weirdness. Then again, it is a very comfy sofa. Any adult bull walrus of average intelligence, caught far from home and in need of a kip, would find it a congenial spot for the night.

On closer inspection, the slumbering form turns out to be the Guvnor, whose pub is only a hundred yards down the road, i.e. a lot closer than the Alaskan peninsula, where walruses abound. This is still odd, though, a reversal of the natural order of things. Is it not I who is meant to pass out in his pub, and not the other way round? As I prepare my morning pot of Assam with shaking hand, I realise that some reconstruction of the previous evening is called for. The situation is, I suspect, rather like that at the beginning of the popular comedy film *The Hangover*, which I have not yet seen. Everyone says I should see it. Even my children say I should see it. Why? I cannot imagine.

Gradually, the jigsaw assembles itself. The evening begins, I now remember, with the arrival of a friend of my friend Amel. The soul of generosity, Amel once absented herself from her own tiny flat in Paris so that I and the Woman I Love could stay there. She has called to ask if a friend of hers can stay in the Hovel for the night and it would be mean-spirited to refuse.

The friend is a charming Oxford graduate called Emmanuelle, in London for an interview. I pour her a glass of wine and she warns me that she's 'a bit of a lightweight', words which, when recalled at two thirty in the morning as she accepts another glass of Razors' Lagavulin, ring a little hollow. But I am getting ahead of myself here. The most startling thing about her, it turns out, is that she is having an *affaire* with the son of a porn baron and owner of — Newspapers and Channel —. The young have opportunities denied to the middle-aged, don't they?

Like so many young people these days, she has no trouble conversing with a horrible old ratbag like myself, and if she feels at all awkward, she conceals it. It is at this point that Razors texts me to say he is bringing a 'nice girl' back, 'who might be your new flatmate'. For some reason, I feel a deep sense of foreboding. Justified, it turns out. This so-called nice girl is, looked at one way, very nice; in the sense of being outgoing, cheerful, and extremely easy on the eye, but after about three seconds in her company it becomes quite clear that she is unsuitable flatmate material. After a little bit longer, I reflect that even living in the same city as her makes me feel slightly uncomfortable, and it is well that London is a place one can readily hide oneself in. I thought that age and experience had inured me to the varieties of female insanity, but Julia (for that is her name, and I'm not going to change it, because of my public service obligations) manages to raise even my eyebrows. In fact, when my new friend and I join her and Razors at the Duke, even the Guvnor looks scared, and he's seen *everything*.*

So I find myself at a bit of a loss when the doorbell goes at about midnight, and I find the Guvnor himself at the front door, looking a little sheepish and carrying a fullish bottle of Rioja. He has apparently locked himself out of his own pub. It is, I see, turning into one of those nights. Why is it that people descend on the Hovel en masse like this?

---

* Many times since I have been asked to describe exactly what she did that was so alarming. All I can reply, to this day, is that it is not so much what she did – I mean, everyone's allowed to dance on the table and play with knives when they've had a few – as the look in her eyes as she did these things. Months later, the memory of this look is enough to make me go cold inside, and consider the lucky escape I had. Later on, when Razors and I are reduced by geographical distance to conversing via Gmail chat, I mistakenly type 'blady' when I mean 'lady'. However, as we both realise instantly that the word 'blady' is a perfect neologism to describe the kind of woman who might go after you with a knife if you spurn her in some way, the term sticks, and I would like the compilers of future editions of the *OED* and other reputable dictionaries to recognise me as the coiner of this horribly useful word.

And I am not accustomed to such nights these days. The previous week had been spent in domestic bliss in Cambridge with the WIL: early bedtimes, early awakenings, with me doing my two thousand words a day, preparing food and making sure the kitchen was spotless before she got back from work. I *loved* it. And now I am imprisoned in the small hours, having to contain a demented thirty-year-old South African and wondering how long it will be before Razors stumbles onto the terrace with the business end of a pair of scissors buried in his back.

Three years ago, when I arrived in the Hovel, this kind of thing happened all the time, and, for some reason, with increasing frequency once Razors moved in. But I am now older and maybe even a little wiser, and I cannot remember the last time I had an evening like that. And I can honestly say that I don't want another one like it for a long time. I grow old . . . I grow old . . . I shall wear the bottom of my trousers rolled.

*

I wake up at 7.30 a.m. feeling fine. This is never a good sign and, sure enough, by about noon I am feeling rotten. Ho ho, I hear you snigger, Lezard has been at the happy juice again (what the South Africans call 'vineyard flu'; or, as the Aymara of Peru and Bolivia say: *umjayanipxitütuwa* – 'they must have made me drink'). Well yes, all right, I have, but no more than usual, the standard iron rations of a bottle a night. Let us get one thing clear: it's not too much. I remember mentioning on my first night in Marylebone to Guy the Millionaire, the second friend I made in the area after moving into the Hovel, that drinking a bottle of wine a night was one of the reasons Mrs Lezard chucked me out. 'And then what?' he asked, baffled. Guy made his squillions himself, by the way, and with the non-handicap of a hearty appetite for lunch to boot, and looks and acts how Alan Sugar would act if he were a nice human being. Niceness etches itself on the face, as well as evil. And I was heartened to read a letter in the 'Last Word' section of that excellent magazine, the *New Scientist*, from a man who had drunk an average of a bottle of wine a day for over thirty years with no ill effects. No readers, in their replies, called him an alcoholic, suicidally reckless, or immoral. They largely said, 'Me too.'

Anyway, I am feeling poorly with something that feels nothing like a hangover: the dizziness and fatigue that is the hallmark of the lurgy. I have to spend the day with the kids and am even more useless with them than usual and by the time I get back to the Hovel I am half dead. I watch *EastEnders* with Razors in an uncomprehending trance and go to bed at eight thirty with a glass of tonic water. I do actually feel just about well enough for a glass of wine but think – hey, why not give Mr Liver a break for the evening? I'm sure he'll appreciate it, and it might reduce the circumference of my belly by a millimetre. Carried on over several weeks, I might lose it altogether. (At the moment I look pretty much as I did a year ago, apart from slightly greyer hair and a protuberance that makes me look as though I am in the early, but visible, stages of pregnancy. My daughter has taken to laying her hand on it in silent rebuke, or – perhaps – as a gambler might touch a bald man's pate for luck.)

I am also glad to discover that I am not actually an alcoholic, in the sense that I do not develop the shakes or start hallucinating. I have given up alcohol before, for a month, after a disastrous escapade on a hen night in Amsterdam, in which I was the only male present. This resulted in my having to be literally wheeled back onto the plane (sprained ankle, in case you're wondering) and an ultimatum from Mrs Lezard to stop for a month or be kicked out. I managed the month rather more easily than I thought I was going to, although I did find the evenings dragged on a bit. (Apart from the time we watched *The Matrix* on video and I had a little dope: I began to accept the film's premise as an extremely plausible explanation for everything, and didn't dare touch any mirrors for a bit in case they went all sticky and shimmery and allowed me to pass my hand through them.)

And so the evening did what prior experience has taught me they do under such conditions: it dragged on a bit. I recalled that I had actually gone thirty-six hours without booze recently, and found sleep impossible to fall into easily because I spent half the night worrying about the wiring in the Hovel, and whether the place would burn down as I slept, if I were ever to sleep. Say what you like about the fruit of the grape, it certainly stops you from freaking out about your electrics. I read a lot: about half of the *Purgatorio* and a volume of Clive James's memoirs, which are of course infallibly entertaining but always leave me with an acute and debilitating awareness of my own failure. I remember when a friend of mine, notorious for his alcoholic and chemical intake, started on an admirable life of total sobriety, and he recommended it on the grounds, among other things, that it increased the mental bandwidth considerably. Imprisoned in my head, I found no similar benefit whatsoever, apart from a step up in the level and intensity of fruitless speculation: why have I not got round to doing my accounts? Why have I achieved so little? Am I too free and easy with accepting friend requests from Facebook? What's going to happen to me when they stop paying writers? Are my children going to be happy and fulfilled members of society when they grow up? Is Test match cricket ever going to be free-to-air again? What's going to happen when the ice caps and the permafrost melt? And why does my pee sometimes smell of Sugar Puffs *even when I have not eaten Sugar Puffs?*

I wake up the next morning feeling like shit, as usual. On the whole, the experiment has been a success, if not an unqualified one, but I think it'll be a while before I try it again. And my pee still smells of Sugar Puffs.

*

Funny to be back in Cornwall for my summer holidays for the first time since I was a child. I do not know what upturn in the family fortunes was responsible for the decision never to return, for there has been no significant upturn in the family fortunes that I have been aware of, unless it is simply the passage of time, but I do remember the annual ritual of my father pacing up and down in the laundrette in Delabole, saying 'Never again' in a voice loud enough for anyone to hear, while the skies wept beyond the steamed-up windows. There was a year when this ritual went unobserved due to freak good weather, and we all obscurely felt its lack.

But Cornwall is a place of deep past, in itself and for me. The Woman I Love rebukes me, correctly, for my mute but obvious disappointment with the newly built, characterless holiday block we are staying in, reminding me that it is all we can afford, but I am also spooked because I have been driving back into my own childhood. I remember one year when the Watergate scandal broke and my mother, American, was glued to the news for the entire fortnight. I became almost certainly the best-informed ten-year-old on American politics in the country (I can remember the names of the conspirators the way I can remember almost the entire Arsenal team from the wonderful 1970–1 season) but I was confused when we saw signs to a town called 'Watergate' only a few miles away. So the place certainly made an impression on me, which has sometimes worrying resonances for when you are supposedly grown up. The child is father to the man, and like a stern father, its frank gaze can be unsettling. When you bump into your own childhood you can't help but wonder if the child, bumping into you, might not reasonably ask: 'Is that the best you, or I, can do?'

Well, at least I have learned not to take a cat on holiday. Freakishly, even by the standards prevailing among the more ailurophiliac inhabitants of the British Isles, we would take both of ours, which tested everyone's patience, both humans' and animals', on the then nine-hour drive. It was nine unforgettable hours each time, but was apparently preferable to the anguish of leaving them in the hands of strangers. One of the cats shot out of the car when we stopped for a pee or car-sickness break on Bodmin Moor, and each family member had to stand guard on each side of the Rover with a shrimping net while the miserable animal crouched beneath the ticking chassis. I still sometimes wonder whether anyone in the passing traffic interpreted the scene correctly. And was it later on, or on another journey, that my brother and I had to press ourselves against the car doors to avoid the lake of cat diarrhoea spreading over the back seat? Either way, the car never really smelled the same again, and in the end my parents, finding it unsellable, passed it on to me. And even though I was the only eighteen-year-old I knew with unrestricted access to a crimson Rover P6 2000, I never managed to seduce anyone on the back seat.

But back to the present day. I am now becoming acclimatised to our holiday home. Like a cat, it takes me a couple of days to get used to a new place, after which I am reluctant to leave. Give me a dressed crab and a chilled bottle in the sunshine and I'm happy. It's also interesting to see how the surface of the landscape has changed. There's a copy here of Daphne du Maurier's *Vanishing Cornwall* and she's fretting in 1966 that it will become 'the playground of all England, chalets and holiday-camps set close to every headland', and indeed the Cornish have been known to take a pragmatic approach to the exploitation of their countryside; if I step on to the balcony and turn to my left, I see nothing built before 1990, at a guess; to my right, there's nothing very inspiring, and as for Newquay, a couple of miles down the road . . . well, it's a horror. But Padstow, although overrun by emmets such as myself, and in Rick Stein's thrall, is still pretty, pretty enough to make one think of settling there out of season, were it not for the price of real estate, which rivals Kensington; and Port Isaac is, once you get into the middle, unchanged, as higgledy-piggledy as Fes, and whose cave, on the right-hand side as you face out to sea, is still as cosily thrilling to explore as it ever was. (It goes just far back enough for a child to feel brave when she touches the back of it, and entertain the possibility that there might be buried treasure somewhere within.)

And not all changes are for the worse. When I was last here a surfer was an outlandish novelty – no one had ever seen one in this country outside the credits of *Hawaii Five-0* – but now you can't move for them, and you see them padding around town in their wetsuits and bare feet when it's pissing down with rain and there aren't even any waves on the beach. But I like the mentality of the surfing subculture, which encourages a kind of dopey friendliness, and if this also means there are more extravagantly decorated VW camper vans than I remember from my childhood, then that's fine. And if the price of the wines on sale in Rick Stein's deli may make you question the notion that Cornwall is the place where you go on your hols when you don't have much money, it is still the place where Tintagel is, where Camelot might be, and where King Mark waited for Tristan to bring the princess Iseult back from Ireland. Which is good enough for me.

*

I write this on the third year, to the day, of my arrival at the Hovel. Three years of living as I please – which, actually, as should be abundantly clear by now, is not at all the same as how I want to live. How am I going to celebrate this auspicious anniversary? At the moment I'm thinking of clearing out the fridge. I've been away for eleven days and during my absence something, I know not what, has taken advantage of the relaxed vigilance and decided to crawl into it and die. The smell is so bad it has even got into the eggs which I cooked for my breakfast this morning. It is so bad you can smell it in the rooms upstairs even when the door has only been open for a few horrified seconds. And the freezer . . . I will not dwell too long on the freezer. Even though the door to it is shut, opening it and peering within suggests the kind of sinister Antarctic hell depicted in *The Thing*, specifically the 1982 remake by John Carpenter, itself a flawless masterwork of horror, but not the kind of film you want to be reminded of in a domestic situation.

But even though I had been vaguely looking forward to coming back to the Hovel after Cornwall, I find myself instead suffering a severe attack of the post-holiday blues, and it is, through no fault of her own, not entirely alleviated by the instalment of the new inhabitant, Emmanuelle, the friend of a friend who came to stay the night, liked the look of the place, and moved her stuff in shortly afterwards. We get on splendidly and she is a pleasure to have around, and it is nice to be tacitly considered an acceptable person to live with. But something else is niggling away at me. Perhaps after such a long time with the Woman I Love, who works hard to maintain a lifestyle characterised by decency and sound organisation, and would no more allow her fridge to get out of control than I would allow myself to use an emoticon or the abbreviation 'lol' in a text message, I have become a little disenchanted with Bohemian squalor. And I have the strange mixture of feeling trapped, but with nowhere else to go. The emptiness of the place is unsettling, too. Not even the memory of Richard Madeley giving the WIL the glad eye in Tintagel, despite my brooding, Heathcliff-like presence, is a consolation. (Once you get the likes of Madeley ogling your partner you realise you have reached the big league of something or other. I toyed with the idea of emptying my pint over his head, which would have made the news, and not only in Tintagel.)

No, celebrations are not in order, and not just because I seem to have picked up an ailment which mimics the symptoms of rheumatoid arthritis and has me walking about the place like a very, very old man. Razors is away until Monday and besides, contrary to what I wrote here not too long ago, I am going to stick with my new no-alcohol-during-the-week-except-perhaps-for-just-the-one-glass-of-wine-to-soothe-the-nerves rule,* which, along with the diet the WIL and I have thrashed out together, should see my David reduced to a tolerable size within a month. (David: *n. sing.*, a term coined by myself in reference to my friend David T——, used to describe a pot or beer belly, which has been taken up by all my friends, and my friends' friends, and should go nationwide within the year, if its popularity as a term continues to grow at this rate.) I see no improvement after a day or so but I suppose these things take time.

Yet the depression I feel on return from holiday has taken me by surprise. It is partly due to my impending fear of the winter. I know I am writing this in bright Indian-summer sunshine but this is only a cruel ruse on the part of the weather gods intended to bring home to us what it is we are going to be missing for the next eight months. As you get older you get more sensitive to the change of the seasons. This is fine in spring but not when the days wane and the darkness starts encroaching. There is also a deeper,

---

* This is not a rule that was enforced for any meaningful time at all, I have to admit. But then you hardly needed me to tell you that, did you?

more existential element to my disenchantment, and that is contained in the very word 'holiday'. It is also, by way of metaphor, contained in whatever it is that has contrived to stink up my fridge, which may as well have stuck a note on the door saying: 'The smell you will experience on opening me may as well be a symbol for the Augean stables of your existence.'

I had always thought, perhaps smugly, that I had contrived to make my life one long holiday – certainly people I know who have real jobs in offices and the like envy the fact that I can get up when I want to – but it isn't really like that, or not so much like it that it is enviable. Everything has to be done oneself, and what with the backlog of work, the books to read and think about, the book to write, the accounts to do (my adviser tells me that my only hope is to go to the accountants and simply present them with the enormous plastic bag full of receipts, and tell them to get on with it), the child support to pay, the holiday laundry to do, and the fucking fridge to clean, it looks as though I have my work cut out for the foreseeable.

*

A pint? asks Razors, and so we slouch off to the Duke. I don't really feel like a pint – we've already had a couple of bottles of Shiraz between us – and besides, it's going to interfere with my stomach-reducing plans, but Razors is only here for another week or two, it's a nice evening, and who knows when, if ever, we'll be able to do this again? Anyway, my not-drinking-during-the-week resolution has been a complete failure, so I don't see why I should start getting all fussy now. I blame Razors. He came back after three weeks on the other side of the Atlantic and still thinks it's five hours earlier than it actually is. I thought another game of night cricket might calm him down but all that happened is that he tied me up with an inswinger so vicious it made me fall over; three days on I still have an ugly bruise on my left shoulder. We managed to excite the interest of the police again; not a helicopter this time, but a squad car. They couldn't have been sweeter about it. There had been complaints, we were told, but I figured the senior officer liked the game himself and suggested he have a go. To his great credit, he admitted he was rather tempted, but thought that on the whole he'd better not, and that we should go home to bed.

Anyway, in the end, Razors twists my arm, and we do go for a pint, and very pleasant they are, although they do stop serving us at 11 p.m., which isn't really nice of them considering what loyal customers we are. When we get back Emmanuelle is up and feeling like Doing Something. But it is late, and as I have explained beforehand, the nightlife in this part of town is not what you might expect from its postal district. However, one of us, and I have a horrible feeling it might have been me, says, in a quiet voice full of doom, 'There's always Sophisticats.'

Sophisticats! The very name sends a tremor through the room, particularly through Razors' substantial frame. This, lurking beneath a multi-storey car park which itself lurks guiltily behind Oxford Street, is the local place for getting charged a bomb for drinks while ladies in their underwear dance for the weary businessman. (I had thought to change this establishment's name for legal reasons, but (a) I'm not going to say anything nasty about it, or nothing that's not already in the public domain, and (b) how can you come up with a better name than 'Sophisticats', or get a better idea of the louche pleasures it affords with something else? The name 'Spearmint Rhino' has, as far as I'm concerned, fallen at the first hurdle when it comes to conjuring up images of lightly clad women cavorting for men's pleasure, and was presumably only chosen because it's the kind of word-combination which does well on a Google search.*)

Emmanuelle likes the sound of the name 'Sophisticats', and repeats it in the kind of voice which makes

---

* Research tells me I am wrong. I have since discovered that, unless one of Wikipedia's contributors is playing a cruel joke on the kind of person who looks up 'Spearmint Rhino' on Wikipedia, a plausible eventuality, it seems that Spearmint Rhino is actually an offshoot of an existing restaurant chain called Peppermint Elephant; which, frankly, gets us nowhere.

Razors really, really want to take her there. Well, it is nice to know she is not a prude. Or drunk. Or both. But I do wonder what on earth could possibly be going through his mind.

So off we stagger to 'London's Premier Gentleman's Club', as, understandably, it chooses to misleadingly describe itself (the word 'premier' here allows for a certain amount of wiggle-room in interpretation, and I choose my words carefully). On the way we establish a few ground rules. One: Razors is paying for our entry, and our drinks, every single one. He is about to get a job paid so well it makes me want to throw up, and I'm stinking broke, as usual. Two: He will, however, not pay for any lapdances, except for his own, and, I strongly suspect, although this goes unspoken, Emmanuelle's, unless it is with a man. This is fine by me: being in love with someone else, and properly this time, I have no desire to have a woman I do not love writhe all over me, not even in her underwear. It never seemed like much of a great deal in the first place, though, and the attraction of such venues has always mystified me. I have known men who have blown thousands – I do not exaggerate – in one night at places like this, which seems to me the perfect example of how to exploit the person with more money than sense. One can contrive such delights at home simply by making a tasty dinner and then asking nicely. Still, here we go, and I have the strange sensation, once again, of having stepped into a novel from the 1930s or 1940s, either one by Wodehouse featuring what must be the best name for a dodgy club ever devised, 'The Mottled Oyster', prone to police raids, or the kind of sleazy joint described by Evelyn Waugh when he wants his characters to have an evening they will regret for ever.

And so we descend into the infernal regions, Razors having been relieved of sixty-odd quid so that we can experience the privilege of passing the bouncer. (Who, it must be said, raises an eyebrow at Emmanuelle, for she does not seem to have been coerced into joining us, or suffering from a touch of the Rohypnols.)

Inside all is plush and red and filled with women mooching about in their underwear, trying to attract the attention of the men they outnumber by about two to one. Razors orders a bottle of pink champagne from a cuvée hitherto unfamiliar to me, and we drink. He ogles, Emmanuelle looks about her, fascinated, and I scowl. This place would be very unlike my cup of tea even if I were in a good mood, and I am not. (An inexplicable *froideur* has arisen from the direction of the Woman I Love, like the first hint of autumn, or an oncoming storm.) The only thing cheering me up at the moment is the knowledge that Razors is going to be stiffed for the bill. Eventually even we are approached by a woman in her underwear. The one who sidles up to me is blonde, and quite pretty, but I am not in the mood. I make a speech the precise wording of which I forget, but which went pretty much like this:

'Sorry, love, but I'm not in the mood. This kind of place makes me sick and I feel terrible that you have to work here, humiliating yourself for a bunch of disgusting, mindless cunts. If you want to have money shoved in your knickers then you're wasting time with me, I'm afraid. I'm sure one of those morons over there' – I gesture to the other side of the (surprisingly small) room – 'will be more than happy to oblige.'

She gives me a funny look, and departs.

A few minutes later, another woman comes over and I repeat my spiel.

This time she does not leave. She blinks once or twice, and then tells me that this is an unusual speech for a punter at Sophisticats to make; she, certainly, hasn't heard anything like it before. This saddens me more than I can say.

We then get into quite a nice conversation, during which I ask Razors to buy more of that pink 'champagne'. My new companion refuses a drink, perhaps wisely, and I tell her what I do, and what my name is in case she doesn't believe me. I rant a bit more about the iniquity of such places, what they say about the men who get off on or indeed in them, and the system which makes working in them an option for women who, say, are trying to raise children on their own, as is the case with my interlocutor. Strangely, the management throw neither of us out. In the end I shake her hand courteously and bid her farewell. I am starting to see double and it is time for me to go to bed. I walk Emmanuelle back – it's 4 a.m. and, besides, she's unsure of the way – leaving Razors to pluck the gowans fine on his own. Let the dice fall where they may. An instructive evening, then – but I'm never, ever going back, not even if Razors is paying.

*

I have just come back from a lunch at St John, the splendid restaurant in Clerkenwell which serves up bone marrow and other bits of animals that the English normally eschew. In the old days, I would not have been able to write a sentence beginning 'I have just come back from a lunch at St John' without it taking me half an hour of tiresome rewriting. In fact, I would not even have attempted anything so complex. Lunch at St John – or the other favoured venue when I could get publishers and agents to stuff me with food and drink, the Quality Chop House in the Farringdon Road – used to be a luxurious affair. I would tend to get there ten minutes early, so I could grab a glass of champagne, to be put on my host's bills, on the sly. When my date, or meal ticket, arrived, I would then have a big dry martini. I think a restaurant stands or falls on the quality of its pre-lunch cocktails, don't you? Then there'd be a bottle of something white to go with the first course. Then there'd be a nice bottle of claret to go with the main. This would tend, if I had any say in the matter, to disappear rather quickly and so we'd have another one. Then there'd be a half bottle of dessert wine to go with the pudding. Then I'd order an absolutely enormous Armagnac to go with a teeny-weeny coffee, arriving home at about six and ready for the pre-dinner bracer.

That is how lunches are meant to go in a cleaner and better world, but *tempora mutantur, nos et mutamur in illis*, and the person buying me lunch is a writer, not an agent or a publisher, so even if I'd been in the mood for a *grande bouffe*-style blowout I wouldn't have wanted to stiff a novelist for the tab. This is also a kind of working lunch: Tom McCarthy, for it is he, Booker favourite and chair of the International Necronautical Society, and I are thrashing out some details about the interview I will be conducting with him on stage at the South Bank later in the month. By a strange coincidence, I'm also chatting with Howard Jacobson at the Hampstead and Highgate Literary Festival in the same week. I dunno. You wait years to be asked to interview a Booker shortlistee and then two come along at once. I am normally highly averse to this kind of thing, especially after what happened at the Cheltenham Literary Festival in 199something, when I interviewed Alex Garland and Nicholas Blincoe in front of five hundred people while half covered in mud. (Long story.) But Tom and Howard both requested me specifically and, even though the former's latest got something of a spanking in the very magazine I write for, I am a fan of both authors and it's an honour to oblige them. And Tom himself is delightful company. Conversation between us tends to revolve around Tintin, Samuel Beckett and cricket, which means we could go on *ad infinitum*.

Later on, I get an email from a publicity person from Cape. She says she understands that I had a lovely lunch with Tom McCarthy and invites me to join the Cape team for the Booker Prize dinner. This is, I feel, something of a result. My feelings about the Booker are mixed. Despite being probably the only person in the world who makes what could loosely be called a living from reviewing books, and having done so full-time for twenty years, I find myself a little peeved that I've never been asked to have anything to do with the prize. My official position on this, and this is not too far from my unofficial position, is that having to read two hundred contemporary novels in three months is not my idea of fun, and I am glad to have dodged that particular bullet, but in my heart of hearts I know that this is sour grapes and it would be nice to be asked, even if it's just so I can say no thanks. (The workload of a Booker Judge really does sound Stakhanovite. And that's just opening the Jiffy bags. Imagine what a strain it would be if they read the books.) So being asked to don the black tie without having to go to the trouble of writing or judging any novels sounds pretty good. I nonchalantly email the first Mrs Lezard asking if my DJ is still at the family home. I know the whole business of dressing for dinner is ridiculous but it appeals to my inner Bertie Wooster and, besides, I take a smug satisfaction in being able to tie my own bow tie. And, as I contemplate my new-found respectability within the literary world, I find my smug satisfaction soaring to dangerous levels. Even the nagging fear that I may not be able to fit into the DJ doesn't worry me. After all, it is perfectly acceptable these days to go to black-tie bashes in a terrifically daring ordinary lounge suit, thus demonstrating one's devil-may-care attitude to social conventions.

In the end, it turns out that 'there has been some confusion' at Cape's end and that they don't have a place for me after all. The turnaround has been rather swift but at least the natural order of things has been restored. I feel less Bertie Wooster, more Charles Pooter. Although even he managed to get invited to the Mansion House Ball.

*

Razors has gone. How long he will last in New York is anyone's guess – Americans are not the tolerant, easy-going people they once were – but I wish him well, blast him. This means, though, that he needs a replacement.

How do you replace a forty-seven-year-old borderline alcoholic who makes groaning noises at Samantha Janus on *EastEnders* and understands the rules of night cricket? Not easy. In the end I have decided to replace him with two girls barely into their twenties.

This is not, I hasten to add, the dream situation you may lazily think I think it is. One of them is, of course, Emmanuelle. The other, and this is where things get tricky, is the daughter of the Woman I Love, who is also, at my instigation and suggestion, going to start work at the Duke.

The overlap between Emmanuelle and Razors has been most diverting to behold. Razors, for reasons too complex and private to air in these pages, has been suffering from a period of celibacy lately. So when he rummaged through the DVD collection and picked out Buñuel's *Belle de Jour* as a film we could all watch together, I wondered whether he was thinking things through properly.

As those of you who have seen this film will recall, it is a masterpiece of eroticism which says disturbing things about male and female desire. It also spoke deeply to Razors, who kept glancing furtively at our new housemate, curled up on the sofa as demurely as Catherine Deneuve. After a while the atmosphere in the room thickened, and I could see that Razors was suffering profound inner turbulence, like a kettle on the point of boiling. Even though the evening was autumnal, I could actually see beads of sweat forming on his pate, which he had to wipe off every few minutes. When Emmanuelle left the room, he shoved his fist into his mouth and bit his knuckles until they bled. When she came back and casually mentioned that a man in the street had tapped her on the shoulder and said, 'You have amazing legs; can I have your phone number?' Razors left the room, saying something about having a shower, in a strangled voice.

Being properly in love with someone else, and therefore blind to the charms of all other women, I can take a detached and amused attitude to all this. And it is nice to fall into the role of avuncular elder statesman. 'What's the Groucho Club?' she asks. 'What does "on the game" mean?' (Cue more knuckle-biting from Razors. I do hope his self-control, rudimentary at the best of times, holds out until his departure.)

But when the daughter of the WIL arrives in a few days, we enter uncharted waters. Maybe readers out there will be able to help me. Is there any precedent to this situation in art, literature, history or folk memory? The story of two disreputable separated men of a certain age living together is one as old as comedy, but one divorced man and two twenty-year-old women, one of whom is the daughter of the woman he is stepping out with?

The first problem, as I see it, is the wall between my bedroom and the one next to it. It is not thick.

Through it, one can hear the murmurs of people talking in their sleep, or be able to tell whether they are scratching themselves with the end of a pencil or their fingernails. When the wind is in the right direction, I fancy you can hear someone thinking about what they are going to have for dinner that evening. In short, it is not conducive to privacy.

I am consoled, eventually, by the memory of an episode from my own past. I am twenty-two, and very anxious indeed to leave the family home, having finally got a job a year after graduating. A friend of a friend, Jenny Beerbohm, Max's granddaughter-in-law, no less, has a spare living room and sofa in a mansion block in Earls Court. Would I like to stay with her? At the time, Jenny, an ex-model, is in her mid-forties, beautiful, but shy, charming, and kind. 'Is £30 a week too much?' she asks, as we sip our drinks in the Coach and Horses, Jeffrey Bernard giving her the eye over my shoulder. Even on my salary, and in 1985, £30 is practically nothing, and I say yes, barely believing my own good fortune.

I was meant to stay for only a couple of months, but I ended up living there for over two years; I couldn't go until I'd read every book in the apartment, and besides, I was waiting for my landlady to take advantage of me. She never did, but I did learn something about the dynamics of living with someone twice your age who isn't related to you.

The day after I left the 1987 hurricane swept over

south-east England, and the flat above my room collapsed onto my sofa. If I had stayed another night I would have been killed.

Jenny, now, is cruelly dead, as is her best friend, Deirdre, whom I introduced to Jeffrey Bernard, who in his turn immortalised her as 'she who would drown in my eyes'. I mourn their loss often, and miss their friendship, their batty wisdom, their delight in marginal existences, their tolerance and good humour. And how they would laugh if they could see me now.

8

Life in the Hovel continues to be mind-expanding. The first time I was asked what it was like living with two women in their early twenties (is it demeaning or sexist to say 'girls' instead? It's not intended to be; more an indication of the vast gulf of years between us) I thought for a few seconds before landing on a comparison.

'It's . . . well, it's a little bit like Heaven, really,' I said, and I suppose I was thinking of the paradise of the *hashishin*, where the Old Man of the Mountain would recruit his assassins by stupefying them with pot and then releasing them into a garden where the fountains ran with wine and beautiful women ministered to their every need. The literary precedent for my predicament is supplied by a literate friend: the late novel by Donald Barthelme in which a fifty-three-year-old divorced man sets up home with three lingerie models. Its title? *Paradise*. Regarded by critics at the time as below par compared to his other novels, and perhaps not so much a *bona fide* work of imaginative literature as a rather sad piece of wish-fulfilment, it is nevertheless, I am assured, an entertaining read. (I have also discovered, after chatting about this with a hugely distinguished writer the other day, that I have been pronouncing 'Barthelme' wrong all my life.

Check up on the correct pronunciation before you make as much of a fool of yourself as I have.)

Of course, as with everything sublunar, it's not really Heaven, although I do have some fun with Emmanuelle's boyfriend (I use the word in its loosest sense), the son of a multimillionaire porn baron. Gratifyingly, it appears that he is terrified of me, and has taken to sitting in his car outside the Hovel waiting for me to leave so that he can give his beloved another bunch of expensive flowers to atone for his latest outrage. He seems like a nice enough boy but he doesn't look old enough to have sex, let alone drive a car. I have little sympathy for people who can fly off to Las Vegas for a week on a whim, as he did recently, though, and I may have looked rather sternly at him the first time he was summoned into my presence.

'That's funny,' said Emmanuelle after he left, 'I've never seen him like that before. Normally he's really outgoing and boisterous.' The WIL, who has a gift for this kind of thing, came up with a nickname which has, I am afraid, stuck: Pipsqueak. (Oh dear, this does sound rather bad, doesn't it? Let me stress that he really does seem like a nice boy, and when he brings flowers he also brings wine for me, much as one might lull Cerberus into slumber by feeding him drugged honeycakes, as in the *Aeneid*. It works, and the boy can keep doing it.*)

---

* As it turned out, he did not keep doing it, and I can now say

The WIL's daughter has her own cross to bear. After saying that she was too young for him, Darren, the manager at the Duke, has decided that she is in fact just the right age after all, and has taken her under his wing, escorting her back to the Hovel in the small hours. The WIL's daughter is no fool and is also perfectly capable of looking after herself, but the situation is awkward as Darren is her employer. He, too, seems to be acting like a gentleman but I've seen that look in a man's eyes before, quite often in the mirror: he's smitten, poor thing. (Meanwhile, the Duke has problems, too. A car drove into it in the small hours last Sunday morning. I asked the Guvnor if he'd been keeping up his payments and he just muttered something non-committal. The WIL also noticed that two of his front teeth were missing. Obviously something funny is going on.)

But it is strange, to find oneself *in loco parentis* to two young women without actually having any parental powers. All one has is anxiety. The first night the WIL's daughter started work at the Duke I waited until half past one in the morning for her to come back; in the end I tiptoed down to the pub (paus-

---

that maybe he wasn't quite as nice as I thought. Apparently being the son of a very wealthy man has its problems, not the least of which is how hard it becomes to develop personally. If your rich father happens to be a bit nuts, too – think of Ben Kingsley's psychotic gangster in *Sexy Beast* – then so much the worse.

ing only to rap on the steamed-up window of the car where Pipsqueak and Emmanuelle were having their tryst) to make sure she wasn't being chased round the table or worse by the Guvnor. I turned out to be worrying needlessly, thank goodness, but I won't be checking up on her again.

In the end, though, they will gang up on me. Just last night one of them said: 'We were thinking of having a big tidy-up.' I think they want me to get rid of my unsold review copies, of which there are hundreds. Oh dear. So much for Paradise.

*

If no love is, O god, what fele I so?
And if love is, what thing and whiche is he!
If love be good, from whennes comth my wo?
If it be wikke, a wonder thinketh me,
Whenne every torment and adversitee
That cometh of him, may to me savory thinke;
For ay thurst I, the more that I it drinke.
TROILUS AND CRISEYDE

So the weather turns and the days get shorter and the money gets tighter. Still, it's not quite enough. What could be done to make things really miserable? Getting dumped tends to do the trick, so that's what's happened. It happened as I was leaving Marble Arch station after depositing the children back in Shepherd's Bush. This is always a melancholy journey for me, made more so by the weather, and the dead leaves blowing in the wind. There is a voicemail message for me from the WIL: I am to call her. Something in her tone does not cause the heart to leap; rather the reverse. But I brace myself and call her anyway, to be given the following exquisite line: 'I don't love you in the way you'd like me to.'

There are one or two possible replies to this, and I suppress the sarcastic ones, even though, as dumps go, the verbal expression behind this one is particularly weaselly. (Because the last seven words are a pitiful attempt at damage limitation, and dishonest to the fact that there had been long stretches of time when the ways we loved each other were completely congruent.) But never mind: there's never a pleasant way to say this, so I assume an attitude of stoic dignity, even though I fancy I can actually hear my heart breaking as I do so.

I'm getting to be quite a connoisseur of the Dump. There is, of course, the Dump Royale, as effected by the first Mrs Lezard three and a bit years ago. That was achieved conventionally, largely by my own substandard behaviour. Then there's the Dump Petit, as perfected by the Pole, which is achieved by the man making it clear that he doesn't want to have any more children, and constitutes a goodbye shag followed by complete disappearance from one's life. That's the least painful, although it does baffle, and comes back to do so repeatedly in the still watches of the night.

The most painful is the one I'm undergoing now, where you haven't done anything wrong apart from the regrettable incident with the —, which is not anyway considered by most authorities as a dumping matter at all, and you still love someone very much but the other person decides she doesn't love you. I shall spare you further details. Not for the first time, I muse that if love were in fact a drug, the people who made it and the pushers would be hunted down and exterminated without mercy, with myself leading the lynch mob.

So once again life has turned into what Santayana said a life without happiness was: a mad and lamentable experiment. I go to the British Library so as to get out of the Hovel. They don't let you use a pen any more in case you write 'bum' indelibly in the books so each time I go there I have to buy a pencil, as I forget to bring the one I bought before. I now have, I can confidently state, the largest collection of black BL pencils in the world. I sit at the back of Humanities 2, less populated, and face a row of reference books so I don't get distracted by the pretty girls there, whose attractiveness serves only to remind me of what I have lost. I look around sometimes, though, for the nutters. You used to get them all over the place in the old British Museum Reading Rooms, which drew them like moths towards a flame. Now they seem to have gone. I wonder if it's like being the bunny at a poker table: if you can't see the loony in the BL Reading Room, then it's you.

I try not to look like a loony, even if the days are punctuated by enormous involuntary sighs and cries of 'Oh God'. I'm trying to keep my shit together in terms of grooming and exercise (my favourite cartoon ever is by Gwyn Vaughan-Jones and appeared in the *Idler*: a man standing over a vast heap of ordure says, 'I got my shit together – but it was still shit'), but eating still feels a bit unnatural until I succumb to ravenous hunger around midnight.

I look up 'dump' in the *OED*, handily placed virtually at arm's reach. One of the definitions reads 'to export, throw on the market, in large quantities and at low prices', and that's pretty much what it feels like has happened.

I read Kingsley Amis, in the hope of ramping up my misogyny. (On women: 'They used to feel they needed something in the way of provocation, but now they seem to feel they can get on with the job of fucking you up any time they feel like it.' Etc.) But it's not quite taking. Most of my friends are women, the kindest words I've had are from women, and it is possible that while women have got me into this mess, women are going to get me out of it again. Not that I am ever going to believe anything a woman says to me, whether it's 'I love you' or 'It's raining', without checking thoroughly first.

And now it is time to stir. I am all too conscious of the fact that at the time of writing it is 1.40 p.m. and I have only got out of bed to find the notebook in which I put down the definition of 'dump' quoted above. I have to read more Kingsley Amis – and maybe a bit of du Bellay's *Regrets* for extra laughs ('*Heureux qui sans soucy peult garder son tresor!*'), and replace the bedside lamp which, with impeccable timing, decided to kill itself last night, just what the bedridden heartbroken man needs.

Meanwhile, if you, dear reader, have someone to love and someone who loves you, who will look after you when you are unwell and cheer you up if you are sad, who will slip their hand in yours when you walk down the street, someone you are prepared to make sacrifices for and who is prepared to make sacrifices for you, both large and small, someone to whom you can entrust your heart, who in short cares deeply whether you live or die, then give great thanks every single waking minute of every single day, while it lasts. When it stops lasting – well, then you're on your own.

*

There are times when one feels like King Midas's barber, the possessor of forbidden knowledge. In the barber's case, it is the knowledge that the king has ass's ears, the result of ill-advisedly judging a music competition between Pan and Apollo, as I recall (would that some similar divine mockery befall Simon Cowell, you can't help but think). In the end, the barber digs a hole in the ground and whispers his secret into it: but secrets have a habit of coming out, and this is why whenever the wind blows in a field of wheat, the grasses say 'King Midas has ass's ears'.

So I can't tell you the story about how my friend F——, a militant atheist, has started going out with a devoutly religious man. 'Why not?' I ask. 'This is priceless. He even has a beard.' 'Because,' she says, 'it would break ——'s heart.' (—— being F——'s ex-boyfriend. He was pretty rubbish, too, his only skill that I could see watching football on the telly. That said, he did look as though he was really good at that.)

'Damn and blast,' I say, but hold my peace. I know all too well how easy it is to steamroller the feelings of the heartbroken. So to lunch at the Duke for a consoling session with the Moose and a woman we may as well call Mme Depardieu, although she has not yet got round to marrying the celebrated French actor and decorator of planes with his own wee, but she assures us it is only a matter of time (as he seems to be losing his looks and his marbles equally quickly, I would advise her to get a move on). The Moose is very happy as shooting for his vampire film has gone without a hitch. This, I gather, is unprecedented in the history of filming. He has been showing me some photos of the cast and crew on set and taunting me particularly with pictures of the First Corpse, who was to have been played by me. ('He was VERY GOOD,' says the Moose pointedly. He is referring, also, to the time when I baled out of his first promo film; see p.81.) As it is I had been feeling far too dumped to get out of bed, let alone travel to Cambridge for the shoot (for that is where the WIL lives; as it is, I have discovered that going past or even near King's Cross, the terminus for Cambridge, causes unendurable sadness). Although at least my time in make-up would have been brief. Dieters: you can't beat a romantic disaster for weight loss. I hear a very funny story about another critic which I can't repeat, and I pick at my mushroom and polenta risotto, which the Moose calls a girly dish because it doesn't have any meat in it. I think this vampire business is getting to him.

Then again, at least these people are doing something with their lives. Mine seems to have stalled. I have never been exactly the most active person at the best of times, but the last couple of weeks have seen me enter a state of torpor that can only be rivalled by a teenager on his holidays. I was meant to have finished writing a book by the end of October but this isn't easy when you can barely be motivated to stare into the middle distance in an unfocused manner. Thankfully my main job involves reading books and I can still manage to do that, interspersing duty with large chunks of Agatha Christie, whose prose style,

I discover, is wildly variable. ('Mrs Bantry reflected a minute and then applied an urgent conjugal elbow to her sleeping spouse', etc.) What is it about genre fiction that makes it so attractive to those seeking comfort in their distress? I suppose it is precisely the deliberate inability or unwillingness to deal with the deep matters of the heart that appeals. After all, we would, in real life, be pained by someone's murder; when we read an Agatha Christie, we get impatient for the murders. This is literature for those aspiring to the condition of autism. (As for Wodehouse, I am beginning to doubt whether the fabled balm of his stories – even his biographer, Robert McCrum, alludes in his introduction to Wodehouse's ability to stop his readers from killing themselves when in the depths – can work on me when I am in this state. As I mentioned much earlier, I find myself beginning to worry myself sick that the silly romances in his books work out, that love finds a way. His romances, in short, are no longer silly: they have become deadly serious.)

As if in general sympathy with the mood around the Hovel, the toaster dies. Its catching mechanism fails to catch, which seems metaphorically apt. I trudge through the rain to the customer care department of John Lewis. The toaster barely cost a tenner but it had great emotional significance, reminding me of happier days (see p.75). In front of me is a West Indian woman with a fantastically exploded kettle.

She has no receipt but insists that she is under divine protection. When the kettle exploded, she said, the Lord was looking after her, because there was smoke everywhere, the flat could have caught fire, and didn't. She turns to me as if for corroboration. I forbear to mention that if the Lord was looking after her so assiduously, maybe He wouldn't have allowed the kettle to explode in the first place.

The negotiations wear on. The man at the complaints desk, who is beginning to have an air of someone trying to bail out water from a wallowing boat, tries to explain that John Lewis has never sold this particular brand of kettle, which even to my untrained eye, and in its shattered state, does not look like the latest model on the market. The woman is not to be stopped. She buys everything from John Lewis, she says, and something about the way she says it suggests that this, too, is on the Lord's advice. I have to say that were I an omnipotent divinity, or Apollo, or even the Gnostic Demiurge, the semi-competent creator of a botched universe, I too would suggest my people shop at John Lewis, which is never knowingly undersold, and whose electrical goods complaints department caves in after twenty minutes of religiously themed haranguing even when you clearly haven't bought the kettle from them in the first place. John Lewis has come to loom large in my life, through simple geographical accident; when I reflect on how circumstances could so easily have pitched me next to a Morrison's, I thank my lucky zodiac.

When I hand them my toaster they tell me to pick another one of equivalent price off the shelves. I too have no receipt but there is no fight left in them. I am pleased with this new toaster, until, after a week, it, too, breaks down. What next?

*

For what seems like ages, the apartment over the road from the Hovel has been occupied by builders. All sorts of heavy work has been going on: there has been scaffolding, noisy machinery at eight o'clock in the morning, signs saying that hard hats must be worn on the premises. ('That means they're doing structural work,' said the Woman Who Used to Love Me, who knows about this kind of thing.) How boring, I thought, it's going to be turned into an office. How sad it is that people are frozen out of the area because of obscene rents. Boris Johnson, recently in the news for expressing some well-timed sympathy for the underprivileged, is right: there's going to be a Kosovo-style cleansing of the poor, etc. I hate agreeing with Boris about anything but he seemed to be right on the money with that one.

But no. It has been occupied by human beings as a human habitation. To be more precise, it seems to have been turned into a harem. I first noticed the occupants when I saw three young women jigging around to unheard music in the kitchen. They might just have been absurdly happy. In the adjacent room I saw a youngish man, well, younger than me, sitting in an armchair with a beer watching the television. Someone seems to have arranged his life in a satisfactory manner, I thought to myself.

My gaze strayed back to the kitchen. That's a very tight pair of flesh-coloured trousers that young woman seems to be wearing, I thought. I then did a double-take. They weren't trousers, or indeed anything manufactured, at all. She was wearing a T-shirt but apart from that was, as the Irish put it so evocatively, in the nip. And still she and her companions bounced about, making, as far as I could see, a sumptuous three-course meal for the young gentleman idling in the living room.

The lives of others as seen through urban windows are fascinating and erotic, as Hitchcock knew only too well. I too like giving my neighbours a bit of a thrill by brushing my teeth in the buff, safe in the knowledge that the windows facing that side of the Hovel are about a hundred yards away (so they can neither infer my address nor how unattractive I am close up). There was a woman on that side who did the same, presumably for the same reason. You couldn't tell whether she was good-looking or not, you just got the exciting idea of nakedness. It was all in the head, really.

But this lot over the road are driving me to distraction. I've seen them in the local shop and letting themselves in the front door and they are all young and attractive and speak a language which sounds as though it originates somewhere around the Baltic states. The immediate assumption to make is that they are prostitutes but the flat over the road looks far too respectably bourgeois to be a brothel. And there is no hint of anything of that nature going on at all. They once held a party which I thought I'd better invite myself to, just to let them know that they were welcome in the neighbourhood and so on, and that I was master of it, but by the time I'd plucked up enough Dutch courage to ring the doorbell most people had gone home, and the party had reached that half-a-dozen-people-sitting-round-candles stage. At eleven! One is grateful for well-behaved neighbours but sometimes you feel they could be a little more exciting, no?

They're back again as I write this, about half past four on a Thursday afternoon. They seem unfazed by the person staring out at them from his workstation in the living room, although once they did pull the blind down far enough to obscure their faces. But not, interestingly, their bottoms. Now I have never been a peeping Tom, or certainly no more than any healthy heterosexual adult male, but you cannot gainsay the compelling nature of the spectacle. The interesting thing is that they can see me as well as I can see them, and presumably each of us knows this. I suppose their lack of self-consciousness is made up for by my own immense capacity for the same.

A mere eighty feet, at a rough estimate, separates us. And yet how much more than that is the real difference between us? I, too, live with young women, one of whom even cooks for me from time to time, but they don't bounce around like that. I imagine the life of the young man over there and begin to gnaw my liver in envy. He is, obviously, loaded. He is sleeping with at least one of them. People might assume the same about me but one of the women here is the WWUtLM's daughter and the other is, well, busy. She told me the other day that she was in a bad mood because she hadn't had sex for three days. I know the young think the world owes them a living but this is bloody ridiculous. How would she feel, I wonder, if she were in my shoes, i.e. not having had sex for about two months and knowing you weren't going to have any for the foreseeable future?

*

A visit from the young and justly renowned feminist writer, Laurie Penny, who has come for a natter about what it's like being kettled and to watch me drink my customary bottle of Shiraz while she sips from a glass of cider and, later, a cup of tea (like me, and indeed George Orwell, she prefers a good mug of strong tea, made with proper tea leaves). She has a look round the Hovel. Because she is young and is living in the middle of nowhere she is quite impressed by it. Opening the door of the room formerly inhabited by the daughter of the Woman Who Used to Love Me, I am staggered to discover that it is completely empty.

I was well aware that the girl had left, but had no idea that all her stuff had gone with her; I'd assumed this was going to be a painful duty I'd be obliged to help with, out of common decency. But no: it's like thieves have struck in the night, leaving me with a similar sense of violation.

But my main feeling – apart from pity for the poor girl, who found London, and perhaps the whole awkward situation, too much to handle – is one of bafflement. How did she manage it? It bespeaks a formidable level of logistical nous which she had not hitherto led me to suspect she possessed.

And stealth. I've been in the Hovel the whole time, apart from the occasional hour or two per day after school with the kids in the family home, and one evening when I went to my brother's for Thanksgiving. Much of the time has been spent awake, as I have rediscovered insomnia. (The cricket being played in Australia is also playing havoc with the body clock. At the time of writing Australia are 245 all out and I have become fully nocturnal. Such are the dangers of playing back-to-back Test matches.) The rest of the time is spent in bed, not going out and staring at the ceiling or reading. Anyone moving stuff around would have been heard. Also, I would have been quite happy to help, but (and this is another unpleasant thought) it was obviously considered imperative that there should be no further eye contact between myself and any member of the WWUtLM's family. When I tell Razors about this he says they're in league with the devil, an explanation that is not as comforting as he perhaps imagines.

But Lord, how the misery is debilitating. I do manage to make a couple of exceptions to my stay-at-home regime, despite the intense cold. These involve parties, one given by the left-wing publishers Verso, and the other being the *Guardian* First Book Award. It is important to go to these parties as the booze is generally free. They could not have been more different. The former is held underneath the tunnels by Waterloo Station, and is wilfully funky, while the *Guardian* has gone for class and is at the V&A. At the Verso party I start chatting to a writer who strikes me as a decent and amusing man. It turns out that we are both mindful of the fact that the free bar only lasts until eight thirty. (I am also mindful of the fact that the only person older than me at the Verso party is Tariq Ali.)

'Don't worry,' he says. 'I am the Jason Bourne of the free bar,' and it turns out he is not exaggerating. We both arrive at the bar at the same time but he gets served about ten minutes before me and carries off twice as many glasses of Primitivo. Several people lie stunned at his feet but this kind of thing happens to people who stand in Jason Bourne's way.

At the *Guardian* party I run into my esteemed colleague S——, who I thought lived in Paris.

'I thought you lived in Paris,' I say.

'I did,' he says. It turns out that the woman he was with dumped him. I groan in sympathy. And reflect, not for the first time, on the alarming rise in the number of women who decide for no real good reason that their men are not quite right for them, and blithely cast them adrift. Like a social butterfly tossing aside a pair of soiled gloves, as a Wodehouse character once put it. At least I didn't have to move cities when I got dumped. (Then again, I, too, have dumped, and the woman concerned is still, some time afterwards, upset about it, if a recent email from her is anything to go by. The difference is I largely assent to her assessment of my character, and feel rotten about it.)

And the cold is making everything worse. The cold snap may be over by the time you read this but at the moment the chill is Dantean, insupportable, all-penetrating, and another reason for staying in bed. I recall that the deepest part of Hell is, according to the Florentine, composed of ice rather than fire. '*Io non mori' e non rimasi vivo*,' writes Dante; I did not die, and I was not alive. That seems to sum things up perfectly.

*

It will probably come as no surprise to you by now that I have, to put it mildly, mixed feelings about Christmas. On the one hand, it is a shameless capitalist conspiracy which could not have been better designed to humiliate and depress anyone not possessed of comfortable income, stable home life, and secure companionship. On the other hand . . . there is no other hand. I remember my illustrious predecessor in chronicling life on the margins of repectability, Jeffrey Bernard, used to praise the Coach and Horses because Norman refused to put any Christmas decorations up, and not just because he was Jewish – he was also a grumpy sod. I doubt whether he would now find anywhere in the country that served alcohol and was free of festive tat. (You don't even have to serve alcohol to ram Christmas where it isn't wanted. Last October I saw one of those places which offer to cash cheques for the desperate with no questions asked except a hefty percentage; its ceiling was hung sparsely with baubles, and a foot-high plastic Christmas tree adorned the kiosk nearest the window. I do not think I have ever seen anything so miserable in my life.) I haven't been to the Coach for some months now but I doubt somehow whether Norman's tradition is being honoured in this respect. (If it is, I apologise and salute.)

So you will get no sentimental crap about the season here, I'm afraid. Having Christmas jollity forced down your throat when you are feeling fine is bad enough but when you are in the dumps it becomes intolerable, and all the more so because everyone else thinks you're being weird or difficult if you raise any exception or even make a pained face when contemplating the illuminated Santa in your local's window. I remember getting into a terrible argument with Linda, the Guvnoress of the Ux, a couple of years ago. She had gone kind of overboard with the decorations and when she noticed that I had a bit of a scowl on my face while I was having a fag on the step told me to cheer up, things could be worse. At that particular time of my life, however, the only way things could have been worse would have been if I was being assaulted by killer bees on top of everything else – although, come to think of it, they might have provided a welcome distraction – and I gave her to understand this, not in so many words. The resulting chilly mood between us nearly got me barred. We are now the best of friends, and she really is one of the great landladies, but things got pretty sticky for a while back there.

So generally a kind of madness takes people over. You will recall, for it was the most irritating thing ever, with the possible exception of those ads for car insurance, you know the ones I mean, that seasonal advert for Boots which features a group of ghastly women swanning around the place like idiots to the soundtrack of the Sugababes' 'Here Come the Girls'. As a piece of cynically targeted marketing it is flawless, which is I suppose why Boots runs it year after year, or so it seems, and it also seems to encapsulate the spirit of moronic celebration, the celebration of nothing in particular any more except itself, that grips the western democracies from mid-October on. (Or earlier. Selfridges starts officially recognising Christmas in August.) Although I do recall that in Paris, which was for a while mine and the wife's preferred seasonal destination, there was a pleasing restraint about the proceedings, the aesthetic sensibility treated with some respect. I wonder if things are still the same over there. Or has the Christmas cancer spread there, too? There is a ratchet effect to vulgarity, in which each year has to outdo its predecessor in tastelessness.

At which point, dear reader, I suspect I might be boring you. The anti-Christmas rant is itself a traditional feature of the season. If I go on at some length it is not to try and spoil it for those of you who are having a jolly time of it but to offer a refuge and an antidote for those who are being treated by life the way nappies are treated by babies; for those who, when asked, 'What are you doing for Christmas?' have to fight hard to prevent themselves from replying, 'Throwing myself under a tube train.'

At least forewarned is forearmed, although with my romantic situation resembling one of the more grisly scene-of-crime photo walls in TV detective serials, and my financial situation not much better, this promises to be pretty much the worst one yet. This is at time of going to press. (Another aspect of the season that makes it a pain in the aris for even the sunniest freelance writer is that everything has to be written by 9 December.) Who knows? Maybe things will have picked up by the actual day. I have, at least, been invited by my housemate Emmanuelle's mother to go over to the family home in Shropshire for Christmas lunch. It is not Paris, and getting there depends on whether the Estranged will let me have the car, but it is a change of scene, and beats the prospect of sitting in the Hovel waiting for a phone call that will never arrive. There is something appealing about the idea, and such acts of kindness are what the season is all about, or should be.

*

Well, it wasn't too bad in the end – Christmas, that is. Christmas Eve, that was awful, purgatorial, a stomach bug leaving me too ill to do anything but peck at my mother's delicious lunch and huddle under a blanket with the children, and the evening all alone in the Hovel fielding hugely distressing calls from good friends whose romantic situations make my own problems look like a glide through the Tunnel of Love.

So I decide, on Christmas morning, to take up Emmanuelle's mother's invitation to go to Shropshire, even though it's a three-hour drive if you don't stop and there is no traffic and the car doesn't break down. Which, thank Providence, it doesn't.

Shropshire is a little near the Welsh Menace for complete comfort, but, by Heaven, it's beautiful. It has these things which I suppose are technically called hills but compared to the scenery around Baker Street are mountains, and as I leave the ghastly outskirts of Birmingham, twinned with Mordor, I move from Tolkien's imaginarium to C. S. Lewis's, and enter Narnia, as drawn by Pauline Baynes. There is still recent snow on the ground and I clear the head with a stiff bracing walk alongside half-frozen streams.

Being welcomed into a new family can be disconcerting and there is trouble afoot when I arrive: tension between Emmanuelle's mother and her partner, which is resolved by them dumping each other shortly before the Christmas dinner is served. I am impressed by the timing but ambivalent, initially, at my appointed role as Provider of Distraction and Amusing Conversation. (Apparently the final straw, according to Emmanuelle's mother's new ex, was my being asked to help with the potatoes. He has never been asked to help with anything in the kitchen; in fact has always been firmly excluded from it. From this he deduced that Emmanuelle's mother and I were sleeping together, which presents – among many other problems – logistical difficulties of an insuperable order.)

And they are generous. My haul of presents includes a handy clip for keeping one's book propped open, a sign bought in Spitalfields market saying 'NO TRESPASSING/ VIOLATORS/ WILL BE SHOT/ SURVIVORS/ WILL BE SHOT/AGAIN' and a tenderly inscribed copy of Roger Scruton's *I Drink Therefore I Am*, the stupendously right-wing philosopher's digressive and informative book on wine. I may disagree with his politics profoundly but he sure knows a thing or two about wine, and can write about it, too. When not engaged in diverting or amusing people, or playing with the establishment's numerous cats, I find Scruton's book glued to my hands and it is hard to prise me away from it. Emmanuelle had said she'd got me some brilliant presents and she wasn't wrong. It is all very touching.

Boxing Day morning finds me in a good humour. Tom McCarthy, stuck in France without wireless, texts me to ask what has happened in the Test and I am pleased to tell him that Australia have been bowled out for 98. More, or rather less, than that one could not have wished.

And Emmanuelle's family are themselves amusing. On Boxing Day evening we sit round the dining table and have one of the more outrageous cross-generational conversations I have ever had. I don't know about you, but conversations about personal matters when either of one's parents are present tend to be stilted, evasive and quickly and firmly closed down; no such reserve exists among Emmanuelle's family. Her younger sister, or should I say her even younger sister, whom I shall call Lolita, wanders around wearing not much more than a bra and is given to standing behind my chair and giving me shoulder massages, even though in some parts of the country I would be old enough to be her grandfather. Their mother – well, let's just say I shall call her 'Mrs Robinson'. But as both her daughters either are or have been to Oxford you can't say she's been doing anything wrong. Hallelujah: this is a brainy house.

And a somewhat lewd one. Topics of conversation avoid, as I said, the traditional family ones. Lolita, to me: 'If you had to sleep with either me or my sister, who would you choose?' I look to Mrs Robinson for a trace of disapproval but find none. I toy with the idea of saying that until I had slept with both, I would find it difficult to make a decision, but in the end decide this is a little much, and say instead, 'You place me in an awkward position,' as diplomatically as possible, 'but I must say I relish the dilemma.' (I should reassure you that I have no intention of sleeping with either, nor they, really, with me. But still, blimey.) There is a general argument about the relative merits of the shaven and the unshaven female pudenda. (Lolita favours, apparently, the former. I pour myself another pensive glass of wine.) Both sisters express varying degrees of reservation about the merits of heterosexual sodomy. Mrs R. assures them that when the right moment and the right man arrive, such reservations evaporate. Again, a little glass of wine while I think about this. There is more, much more; several times during the evening I find myself wishing I was taking notes. At occasional points one or the other speculates on what it is about me that allows them to be so prodigal with their chat but no one is complaining, least of all me. I suppose I just have that kind of face.

What a nice place. I want to go back.

*

In a surprising but welcome development, Laurie Penny, who popped in for a chat and a look-around a few chapters back, has moved into the Hovel. Once again I find myself in the company of a woman much younger than me. What, I wonder, is the secret of my appeal? Anyway, there is nothing untoward in our arrangements, although there is some prurient speculation from the dirty-minded. These people can take a flying one. For a start, Ms Penny at one point describes me as 'mind-bendingly old'. I know she is exaggerating for comic effect but there is a grain of truth lurking in there somewhere. Secondly, she is already in a relationship. Thirdly, she is a Proper Feminist and would suffer no malarkey even if I were the kind of man who was prone to malarkey. That I pass muster as a housemate with a woman of such principles is actually a source of quiet pride as far as I'm concerned. She also has a fine prose style and we agree deeply on all political matters, although until she empties the bin, I remind her, her position as Feminist Spokesperson for Her Generation is compromised. (Her indignant rejoinder, 'But that's a blue job!' does not, I say, help her as much as she thinks it does.) But she works hard and well and even though I am only slowly getting used to the way the bathroom sink is now more or less permanently stained with pink hair dye, and the tin foil has emigrated from the kitchen to the bathroom (apparently you use it to dye your hair, although I found that I achieved my own grizzled locks entirely naturally, through a combination of three children and perpetual anxiety), the atmosphere of professionalism is catching, and so, in a new spirit of efficiency, I decide to visit my accountant.

I like my accountant. She's jolly and good and she finds my extraordinary financial incompetence amusing. I've only set eyes on her three times, and that over a period of three years, and she has since moved to a swankier firm which, judging by the promotional video they play on a loop in the waiting room, exists only to balance the books of the larger companies or countries about the size of Belgium. I imagine she keeps me on because I make her laugh and remind her of her roots, when she used to look after freelance writers. (Do you remember that episode of *Black Books* where Bernard tries to get his customers to break his arms so he doesn't have to fill in a tax return? He's better at his accounts than I am.)

This time the visit is not quite the usual laff-fest. In the past, they went like this.

Me: Shall we do my accounts, then?

Her: OK, bring them in.

Me: Bring in what?

Her: Your accounts. You know, your expenses and your income.

Me: Can I just give you the password to my online account?

Her (eyes widening in horror): That really is NOT a good idea.

Me: But I don't LIKE doing my accounts, it's boring and makes me cry. Is wine a legitimate expense?

Her: Are you a wine writer?

Me: Not as such.

And so on, once a year. Eventually I agree to do some kind of bookkeeping, which means I buy a pen and an envelope from Ryman's and put the receipt in my wallet and feel as though I've turned a corner, and then I lose the receipt. A year later I go back to the accountant and we repeat the process.

This time I have been very good. Comparatively. I have kept all my receipts religiously for a three-month period. The A4 notebook I bought from Ryman's, the receipt for which I have since lost, looks very impressive on the outside but on the inside, apart from the three months where I have been boring and grown-up, and where all footling purchases which are related to my work are duly noted, I may as well have drawn a big smiley face with the smile part of it upside down. I tell my accountant that it's like this every month, just use those three incredibly well-documented months as an average. She tells me it doesn't quite work like that. There are bent accountants and there are honest accountants and she falls firmly into the latter category. (The best example of the former was the one who told a friend of mine to paint over the rear windows of his car so he could call it a van and therefore claim every drop of petrol and all maintenance as legitimate business expenses. It is a dodge I have contemplated more than once.)

So when she emails me to say she has now done what she can, but I had better come in to discuss it, I get a bad feeling, the kind Douglas Adams and John Lloyd in their book *The Meaning of Liff* called 'an

Ely': 'the first, tiniest inkling you get that something, somewhere, has gone terribly wrong'.

I sit in the offices of MegaCo accountants and watch the corporate video tell me several times how they managed to keep Poland on an even keel during the fiscal year 2009–10. Eventually I am called up. My accountant normally wears distractingly low-cut jumpers but this time she is covered up demurely in black. She tells me that what with me being an incompetent cunt and everything, not that she uses anything like such language, but the import is clear, I now face a tax bill of around this size, and she points to a sum that I could swear is more than News International and Vodafone combined have to shell out a year.

'Is there any way we could get that lower?' I ask, after I spend a few therapeutic minutes blinking.

'Well, you could let me know if there are any more expenses you've forgotten about.'

I even forget to ask her if wine is a legitimate expense. But I do ask if they will send me to prison. To pay this kind of sum, I reflect, I will need, basically, to win the Booker, which, with no plans on my part to write a work of fiction in the immediate future, looks like a bit of a long shot.

My accountant looks at the sum thoughtfully. 'No,' she says after a most disconcertingly long pause, 'I think we can rule prison out. They only send you to prison if you submit false accounts.' But these are false, I want to say, I've left out loads of expenses and yet somehow all my income is in there.

So, in the interests of self-preservation, I try to shift the emphasis of my column in the *Statesman*, so that it will look, to the casual eye, like a wine column. I try this: 'I recommend Chalk Springs Vineyard Shiraz, at £5.49 from Majestic (pre-budget price), an amazing bargain, with deep, rich notes of, er, blackcurrant, toffee, cigar boxes, er, oxtail soup, Benylin and monkey spunk, but in a good way, and indeed the only wine I can afford, so I'll be describing it week after week. Using different words, I hope.' As you can see, it will be a long time before I catch up with Roger Scruton.

*

I write this in a precarious state, on a laptop which may conk out any minute. The socket at the back where the power supply cable goes in has gone wonky: the juice simply isn't getting in. I have a similar problem with the mobile: recharging it involves about ten minutes of fiddling about with the plug and then, as delicately as if it were filled with nitroglycerine, setting it down on a flat surface while it sucks up its electrons. (At the moment it is on the mantelpiece downstairs; I dare not move it for another hour or so.) I have had prior experience of these problems: an old Acer laptop managed to last for ten years, but the last three of them involved an irremediably compromised battery and a socket which only worked if you jammed a match into it, plus up to twenty minutes of agonised fiddling about before it condescended to start. As for the phone, this is apparently a design flaw in the Sony Ericsson, and also in its owner, who whenever asked, 'Which mobile do you want?' replies, 'The cheapest one in the shop, please.'

But I have sympathy with these gadgets. I, too, feel as though I am suffering from an inability to recharge myself. The metaphor is so apt that it seems forced, ridiculous, but there you go; it's also inescapable. Sleep is troubled and never sufficient, however long I stay in bed. And I can stay in bed for a long, long time if I put my mind to it. The other day I didn't haul myself into the world until about four in the afternoon. I spent a couple of baffled hours trying to work out whether this was sloth, depression, or genuine illness. Then when it came for the hour to pour the evening glass of wine I found I could hardly finish it. And if you can't finish a glass of wine then you must be ill, no?

But there is the fear that something has gone irretrievably awry within the body, that something is trying to kill you. And I am reaching the age when a lot of friends are having terrible things happen to them. An old friend has suffered a heart attack, which for good measure has been followed by a stroke, immediately robbing him of his stunningly rich vocabulary and all movement down the right side of his body, turning him into a character from late Beckett (the Unnamable, say what you like about him, was at least the chatty type); and there are too many friends who have been diagnosed with cancer to mention them here even obliquely.

The only bright news lately was about a friend who, what with suffering symptoms it would not be nice to repeat even in these frank pages, was wandering around gloomily convinced he had bowel cancer. And, truth to tell, his diet, a matter largely of red meats cooked *à point* and gallons of booze, and, until a few months ago, a packet of Camels a day, didn't make the prognosis any less likely. So when, after a humiliating and distressing examination, the details of which it would not be nice to repeat even in these etc. etc., it turned out all he had was IBS and what are vulgarly known as bum grapes, there was much relief and even some light teasing.

But I am beginning to feel as though I am living on borrowed time. A study referred to in the *Guardian* last week, and skimmed with a horrified eye, seemed to suggest that air pollution in the middle of cities makes it as likely that one might suffer a heart attack as if one were snarfing up a bucket of cocaine every day. (Perhaps I exaggerate; but that, roughly, was the gist.) One is always prone to a kind of hysterical, superstitious credence in such matters, even though the evidence of one's eyes – people aren't actually dropping like flies in the street – might suggest otherwise. (Actually, I did see someone drop like a fly on the Central Line the other day. I had a send-not-to-know-for-whom-the-bell-tolls moment which might account for my current mood.)

But the most distressing thing happened while I was asleep. Troubled sleep can bring vivid, near-lucid dreams with the texture and cohesion of reality, and the other night I dreamed my life as it would be seen through the eyes of the great cartoonist Posy Simmonds. Let me tell you, if you want to spend the next week feeling like a lowly spotted thing, a creeping beast and a waste of space, try seeing yourself as Posy would see you. In my case I feel exposed: a creature of inordinate and insupportable vanity, idle and degenerate beyond all hope, a self-deceiving wretch who hardly merits the pity, let alone the tolerance of his friends.

Well, at least this assessment, which doesn't really seem that harsh, does allow for the possibility of self-improvement. But, just as with phone and computer, we live precariously. It is all very well saving up one's repentance for the deathbed, but it is not always that we get the chance to die in our beds, or with time to prepare some excuses and apologies. We never know when, suddenly, everything will go dark.

*

The lovely weather combines, unfortunately, with the continuing loss of the shower in the Hovel. One can run the shower if one sits down with it in the bath, and then has a bath, but that is time-consuming, although I have plenty of time to consume, and besides someone, probably me, has finished my bubble bath and not replaced it. Can you have a bath without bubbles? I think not. And so I nip off earlier than usual to the family home prior to picking the Youngest Lezard up from school. The family home has been feeling like . . . like, well, home again, as I have been staying with the entire brood while their mother goes off gallivanting to the South of France for a restorative little break. (Actually, it was York. It's the South of France next week.) I am reminded that looking after three children full time, on your own, is hard work. However, it is also immensely rewarding, as mine are, as I always say, splendid, and better company than a lot of adults I know.

Anyway, what with one thing and another, but mainly the thing about there being no shower and everything below the neck line getting a bit sticky, and everything above it a bit greasy, I decide to help myself to a shower in the family home. After all, I reason, I did pay for it.

Unfortunately, the Estranged Wife had failed to inform me that her new boyfriend was going to be dropping in early too. Now, readers who have separated from their spouses will appreciate that it is hard not to feel a disproportionate degree of disdain for the ex-spouse's new partner. It is hardly reasonable; after all, it isn't the poor bastard's fault. Perhaps it is a way of not feeling contempt for the ex-spouse, or of drawing your contempt's fire. One is bound, unless possessed of almost limitless saintliness, to suspect that the new man in the ex's life is going to be, in some respects at least, wanting; and I am not possessed of limitless saintliness.

So, in short, I have been treating a blameless man with rather obvious nastiness for about six months now. I know, I know. But a recent momentous conversation with someone whose opinion I respect immensely persuaded me of the error of my ways, and I have resolved to act decently from now on.

It is, though, hard to claim decency when one is wet, bollock naked, and taking a cheeky shower in a house in which it would, perhaps, have been best to ask permission to take a cheeky shower. And then I hear the front door being opened, and the tread of someone too heavy and too early to be either a sixteen- or a thirteen-year-old Lezard on the stairs. Then the phone chirrups, and I see a text from the EW: am I, she asks, in the house?

Well, this is hardly the time for me to reply. A man I have been incredibly rude to for some time is coming up the stairs and is going to be entering the bathroom, maybe suspecting that he has caught an unusually fastidious burglar freshening up after a spot of light burgling. He may be armed. Would he have taken the middle child's cricket bat, or will he have one of the lethally sharp new kitchen knives in his hand?

I see the bathroom door being pushed slowly open. I think now might be as good a time as any to start covering up the more intimate parts of the person, and I manage to haul the boxer shorts just past the knees when the ex's boyfriend opens the door to its full extent.

'What ho,' I say. It strikes me that the nonchalant note is the one to go for.

His expression is hard to read, and I must confess I do not spend too much time trying to read it. I see horror, confusion, with notes of disgust and outrage. Doubtless we could have prolonged the moment to discern the exact proportions, but we both seem to reach the same unspoken conclusion: that the bathroom door should be closed, and that right speedily.

Whenever I read the *Guardian*'s version of the Proust Questionnaire in its Saturday magazine, I fantasise about the time when, finally having achieved the recognition I deserve after years of honest toil, I answer its questions and have my answers committed to print. And the question that has always stumped me is 'What was your most embarrassing moment?' Maybe the mind puts my own embarrassing moments into some kind of oubliette, but all I can come up with was the time, forty-odd years ago, when Douglas Green, the notorious shit, pulled my shorts down in front of more or less the entire school. As a refinement, he included my underpants in his grip. (And whatever he says, it was not an accident.) Well, I reflect later over a soothing pint in the sun outside the Duke, I believe I now have a more satisfactory answer to that particular question.

*

A Saturday afternoon. The kids are mooching about in the Hovel, and I am pootling about in the kitchen. It is that null time in the late afternoon, when it is too early for wine, but one has had more than enough tea for the day. In days gone by, this would be when I would call the Woman I Love for a chat, or she would call me, but ever since I got dumped by her, and then, just as it looked as though a reconciliation was on the point of being effected and we were on the brink of returning to something like the *status quo ante*, I had a moment of insanity and slept with someone else while the WIL's daughter was in the room next door, relations between us have been even more on the frosty side than usual. That is, the frost has emanated from one direction only, and with good reason. Anyway, my unpardonable (and indeed inexplicable, unless one counts the sense of dislocation that inspires one to commit the Gidean *acte gratuit* as an explanation) act resulted in both the old- and newfangled forms of rejection: not just complete silence, but that modern refinement, the blocking from Facebook, which is so complete that even if the blockee asks Facebook if such a person as the blocker exists, he receives a negative answer.

Well, so be it, I thought; as Snoopy remarks after a moment of inattentiveness when he loses Lucy van Pelt's balloon, and is last seen walking down the railroad tracks carrying a hobo's bundle over his shoulder: you make one mistake and you pay for it the rest of your life. And one does pay. If being dumped for no reason is bad enough, being dumped for a very good one is much, much worse. Unless one is a Don Juan (pre-Byron) or a de Maistre, scornful of the finer and gentler feelings, the agony of rejection is multiplied, on a logarithmic scale, by the constant awareness of one's own culpability and folly. Nor can one rely on the sympathy of one's friends, except insofar as they realise you are even more handicapped by stupidity than they already thought you were.

Anyway, there I am, getting on with my life, after a fashion, albeit feeling a little emotionally labile as we have all just watched a double bill of *Friends*. (The kids have really got into this venerable sitcom, and have dragged me with them; except now, having seen just about every episode from the pilot to the finale, I realise that the whole damn series is actually about the love affair between Ross and Rachel, and the faint and occasional similarities between Jennifer

Aniston and the WIL don't make the experience of watching it any less agonising. As for the folly of the phrase 'We were on a break!' – that goes through me like a knife.) And the phone rings, and whose name should pop up on the screen but the WIL's?

So, after fumbling with the phone for a bit – funny how panic can make a familiar and normally tractable object feel as though it is both red hot and as ungraspable as a live eel – it turns out she is in town, and wonders if it would be OK to come round. This, mind you, after almost exactly six months of complete silence.

At some point during the long conversation that ensues upon her arrival, she mentions the case of a Brighton man, caught in flagrante by his girlfriend, who agreed to walk through the town holding a sign saying 'I am a cheating c***'.

Now, the town might not have been Brighton, and I may not have the wording on the sign exactly right, but that is not the point. I begin to see what she is driving at.

'A public *mea culpa* is all very well,' I say, 'but I do not think the readers of the *New Statesman* will be particularly interested in the intricacies and vagaries of my love life.'

'Oh, I think they'll be very interested indeed,' she replies. 'How could they not be?' (At which point she goes again through the events summarised on p.271.) 'I'd be interested.'

'But my mother reads the magazine,' I whimper. (This is short for: 'Not only does my saintly grey-haired outspoken mother read that magazine, but there is no way I can emerge from this without forfeiting the last scraps of compassion my readership may retain for me.')

'Well then,' she says.

And there is the dilemma. On the one hand, I am now going to make myself look very bad. And, unlike with Brighton Cheating Man, with no hope of return. (I presume that was why he agreed to his public parade: you don't walk around like that if you think 'Sod this for a game of soldiers.') No, that was made unambiguously clear, and fair enough. On the other hand, if I cannot salute the bravery, kindness, magnanimity and sheer decency of a woman prepared to make friends with me again after all this, then what is the point of being alive, or claiming to be a member of the human race?

Endnote: On legal advice, I have removed the explanatory and partially exculpatory text I wrote prior to this book's publication. Here's another mouse.

9

A Monday afternoon, and I am wondering whether it was wise of me to invite the editor of the *Statesman* to dinner at the Hovel (Laurie, who also writes for the magazine, thinks it's a super idea, but then she is young, has lived in some pretty disastrous places, and perhaps does not realise that the Hovel lacks many of those amenities that civilised people consider as standard, such as a loo seat that doesn't fall off every time you sit on it) when the phone rings. It is the Estranged Wife, calling to tell me that there has been a Cat Incident.

Jaffa, the family cat, so named because she has the colourings of the eponymous biscuit-sized cake, has taken it into her head to jump out of the Velux window in my daughter's attic room without checking to see if this is sensible.

The EW is at work, and for some reason considers her job more important than running around after this cute but demented fleabag. However, she has made an appointment at the vet anyway, because she knows that the daughter and I would never forgive her if the mog, who doesn't seem to have broken anything, turns out to have internal bleeding.

Anyway, I am in full-on heroic mood – the previous day I took part in a record-breaking tenth-wicket stand (72, nearly doubling our score) for that charming team, the Rain Men, even though I was batting with a broken finger* – and even though I am even more skint than usual, I race over to Shepherd's Bush in a black cab. I text the WIL (we are at least on speaking terms again, which is very nice indeed) and she urges me to take the cat to the vet at once. She is at least as nuts about cats as I am, if not more so.

For some reason, Lezards, down the male line in particular, yet certainly including my daughter, are completely soppy about cats, even though my grandmother was debilitatingly ailurophobic (my mother, her daughter-in-law, always made sure that our two cats were in the house when she came round to visit).

Well, we get the cat to the vet just in time for the scheduled appointment, and without getting into too much of a flap about it, and it turns out that everything seems fine, although she is a little overweight, which doesn't have much to do with anything, except perhaps the force with which she hit the ground, and she is in shock, which you or I would be, too, if we had fallen off a roof. At which point the daughter and I are almost hysterical with relief. Even being gouged for £60 for the privilege of watching the vet

---

* This has, of course, absolutely nothing to do with anything else in this book. I just want to make sure as many people as possible know about it.

stick a thermometer up Jaffa's bum and hearing him say she could lose a little weight doesn't seem like too much of a price to pay.

How much of ourselves do we invest in our pets, and why so much? They are our familiars, our tutelary spirits, our household gods, inarticulate repositories of our sense of fortune. If anything bad happens to the cat, it happens to us by extension. When Philip Pullman invented the idea of the daemon, the animal manifestation of the soul that accompanies people in his imaginarium, he was on to something.

Pets are our links with the world, reminders that we share this planet, that our dominion over animals comes with duties and responsibilities. Such as making a fuss over them and buying them boxes of Go-Cat every so often. (I'm not sure why it's called that. Following a quick crap, Jaffa goes straight off to bed after her meal, usually for sixteen hours at a time. It really should be called Stop-Cat.)

The downside of this is that you worry about them almost as much as you do about human beings. In my father's case, more so – even though his cat, whose name is too embarrassing to reproduce for public consumption, is a pampered, truculent snob who has no time for anybody but my father.

I often yearn for a cat in the Hovel, but I would freak out every time I opened the front door, lest it should bolt out into the traffic; I would freak out whenever I went away on holiday (this is a purely academic freak-out, as I can't afford to go on holiday anywhere); and I would freak out lest it should take sick, and perish, or fall off the bloody balcony or something. It is not that funny to think there are sympathy cards to be given to those whose pets have passed beyond the veil. The best one I saw was on sale at an Oxfam shop in Cambridge. It had the words 'Pet Sympathy Card' on the front over a picture of a cute, sad-looking kitten. Inside it said: 'I'm sorry you have a dog.'

*

My birthday. Again. I suppose it is better than not having any more. I have now reached the age Goebbels was when he died, although my achievements are fewer. And, thankfully, not in the same line. Still. I am also twice the age that Martin Amis was when he published his first novel and nearly four times the age Mendelssohn was when he completed the symphony for strings I heard this morning on Radio 3.

Scanning the skyscrapers of review copies in my bedroom, my eye catches, as it is meant to, the title of the latest in Slavoj Žižek's suspiciously unstoppable oeuvre: *Living in the End Times*. End times? Bring 'em on, Slavvy baby. This morning, I found a hastily scrawled 'Happy birthday, Nick!' from Emmanuelle on the back of an envelope intended for the art gallery downstairs and an empty bottle of milk, thoughtfully placed in the fridge door. That would be the handiwork of Laurie Penny. But she did give me a hug a bit later and I can hardly wag the finger when it comes to putting redundant items back in the fridge.

I have to say that this birthday has been somewhat flat so far. One expects this kind of thing as one ages, but this has been one of the most Norfolk-like yet. Then again, I can't expect to repeat 2008's retrospectively hollow triumph, when I walked into the Duke arm in arm with both the Lacanian and Aita (Nigerian, posher than the Queen, six foot three in her Louboutins and, like the Lacanian, a published novelist), the morning after ramming half the pub out with my friends, nonchalantly monitoring the Guvnor's face for signs of incredulous envy. This evening, in 2011, having given them barely twenty-four hours' notice, I will be meeting my beloved little brother and two old friends, and that's it.

But the day drags on, becoming an epic of ennui. I have much work to do but little inclination to do it. Hell, it's my birthday. I sit around, waiting for a phone call and seeing how many Opal Fruits I can eat at a sitting. (Answer: a number bound only by the size of the packet and the indolence, and shame, preventing me from going out to buy more.)

The children, though, have sent me some splendid cards and even the Estranged Wife has wished me a happy birthday, which is nice of her. Perhaps she feels bad about the bafflingly rancorous exchange of text messages we had when I mentioned that HMS *Belfast*'s guns are trained on Scratchwood Services on the M1. (How comforting it is to think that someone in the Royal Navy not only has a sense of humour but feels much the same way about Scratchwood Services as I do.)

What do Scratchwood Services and Opal Fruits have in common? They are no longer called these things. I can see why the Department of Hiding Ugly Truths changed Scratchwood's name to 'London Gateway', but Scratchwood it will remain in the public and private imagination for years to come. Similarly, no amount of social or ethical conditioning will ever get me to say 'Starburst' willingly and on the first attempt. 'Here, have an Opal Fruit,' I say to the children and then add, with a toxic sneer, 'or "Starburst", as they are now called.'

Complaining about the changing of brand names is pathetic. We are far from 'the horror' of existence – Elfriede Jelinek's term, approvingly quoted by Žižek (I had a browse to cheer myself up) – but the marking of another year gone inclines me to morbid thoughts about the passage of time. (In John Moore's immortal line: we're not growing up, we're just growing older.) And hands up, everyone who thinks that Starburst is a better name for Opal Fruits than Opal Fruits. Not only is the impulse behind the change a cynical warping of language, it is a repudiation and effacement of history, the kind of thing Orwell warned us about.

Then again, there is this to be said for these Yahoos and their rebrandings: they remind us that we cannot fight time, even though the endeavour of human culture and art is to put the brake on entropy, to keep what is good of us alive. More Starbursts, anyone?

Then I have a nice drink with my friends and brother; Emmanuelle and Amel ('Hope', in Arabic) call from Paris to sing 'Happy Birthday' to me; Laurie gives me a card whose handwritten message is so touching that I ought to keep it forever; and I get the call I was waiting for. Although, what with one thing and another, life, barring miracles, looks as though it will never be whole again, for when some things get broken they never really mend perfectly again, things don't seem so bad after all.

Author's Note and Acknowledgements

'I have never understood where my life could have been different or how it ought to be justified.'

Guy Debord, *Panegyric*

This book began before I even dreamed it could become a book: I met Jonathan Derbyshire, an editor at the *New Statesman*, at a book launch at Daunt's in Marylebone to which I had not been invited, but which I decided, after a miserable what-can-I-afford?-fuck-all trip to the Waitrose down the road, to crash anyway. After all, as a book reviewer, my main job, I could hardly be turfed out. He asked me how I was doing, and I gave him a brief run-down. I was too uncaringly exhausted, desperate and fed up to simply say 'fine'. I wasn't. I carried on shmoozing and drinking as much free wine as I could, and thought little more of it. But a couple of days later I got an email from the new editor of the *New Statesman*, Jason Cowley, which said, in essence, and about as many words: your column is going to be called, unless you have a better idea, 'Down and Out in London'. Eight hundred and fifty words a week, x pounds per column, doesn't sound much I know, but it's a good rate for us.

Having recently lost a dream job, a ten-year gig

as radio critic for the *Independent on Sunday* – I'd been called by the editor and assured that unless they got someone already on staff, the paper would close for lack of funds – I was now earning less than the most junior of policemen or nurses, let alone my peers. Thanks to my selflessness, the *Sindie*, at time of writing, still exists. One day they will thank me for this. Anyway, I jumped at the chance to make something of my dismal circumstances – and, having before written a column for a few years for the *Guardian* called 'Slack Dad', a grumpy rebuke to the pieties modern fathers were then meant to express, had form when it came to mining my own failures for cash, and there was a certain narrative continuity from Slack Dad to, as I saw it at the time, Sacked Dad.

So the first grateful acknowledgement goes to Mr Cowley, who joins that extremely select company of editors who have said 'You must write a column for us' and actually delivered on that normally nebulous and unreliable promise. I, in turn, have delivered, usually on time, or close enough, for three years, and although the words 'in London' – I liked the Orwellian echo, although I am barely fit to shine Mr Orwell's shoes – have been quietly dropped, the column still runs in that venerable magazine, for which I am proud to write. I took as my model the 'Low Life' column by my old occasional drinking partner, Jeffrey Bernard, whose memory I respect. (That one ran in the *Spectator*, but few remember it started in the *Statesman*.) As I write these words, I am still broke, if not strictly down and out, as I have been at pains to point out in a magazine whose editorial policy is sympathetic to the indigent and deprived; should this book make my fortune, I will relinquish it, with grace, for someone who needs the slot. But I am not holding my breath. These are tough times for writers; even tougher than they used to be. But this is the life I have chosen, and although it might sound as though I am whining in these pages, I would rather this than anything in an office. I may be bad at making beds, and grumble at the unsatisfactory way mine has been made, but I am well aware I am the one who must lie in it, and I hope it is clear that my grumbling is chiefly directed at myself.

My most immediately next thanks are to my editor at Faber, Julian Loose, whose idea it was to modify the first ninety-odd columns into this book; his patience and forbearance, considering he first asked me to write a book in 1997, which I have yet to deliver, are astonishing. Then my agent, Derek Johns, patience and forbearance equally astonishing. To them I owe so much.

As for my friends who have helped me, most are mentioned within these pages, but especial thanks – you really find out who your friends are when things get tough – for meals, loans, drinks, and unmentionable things – go to Toby Poynder, Kevin Jackson,

Kate Emery, Will Self, Hannah Griffiths, Howard Jacobson, Tom McCarthy, Sally Robson, the late Sebastian Horsley, Rialda Sebek, Tina Griffiths, John Moore, Rosa Thurman, Deborah Gnat, Laurie Penny, Caroline Edwards, Aita Ighodaro, Christine Grant, Alan Lempriere, Tony Lezard, Dell Fielding, Ashleigh Lezard, Tom Hodgkinson, Victoria Hull, Antonia Quirke, Karen Krizanovich, Louisa Young, Robert Lockhart, David Quanitck, Meike Ziervogel, Guy Beacroft, Neil Titman, Maria Alvarez, the various staff at the local Majestic Wine Warehouse, and Jed Weightman, who did more good than even he suspected or knew he was doing with his support and suggestions at the outset. My subsequent editors, Kate Murray-Browne and Eleanor Rees, also really saved my bacon as far as making this book acceptable goes. (I can imagine no finer copy-editor than Ms Rees.)

One final word: even though, or rather because, she was the one who ejected me from the family home, the Estranged Wife is really the prime instigator of the whole business, and such asperity as I directed towards her in the original columns, written in the slow- and long-burning heat of resentment, has been, to the best of my knowledge, and happily, removed by me; that unwarming fire is out. For I now, I hope, understand why she kicked me out, and we now actually get on far better than most separated couples in our position. And for her not ever being mean about me to the children, the dedicatees of this book (although I do hope they never read it), for it is, above all, their love and innocent, and not-so-innocent, support that has really kept me alive, I am deeply grateful. I am not really Sacked Dad after all, thank goodness. Many men in my position, and there are many of us, and many less deserving of expulsion than me, have been served worse by their exes. That she has not kicked up any more fuss than a resigned roll of the eyes to the publication of this book does her enormous credit.